Steering Business Toward Sustainability

DATE DUE

JE 10 02			

DEMCO 38-296

Steering Business Toward Sustainability

Fritjof Capra and Gunter Pauli (Eds.)

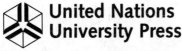

United Nations University Press

TOKYO · NEW YORK · PARIS

United Nations University Press
The United Nations University, 53-70, Jingumae 5-chome,
Shibuya-ku, Tokyo 150, Japan
Tel: (03) 3499-2811   Fax: (03) 3406-7345
Telex: J25442   Cable: UNATUNIV TOKYO

Typeset by Asco Trade Typesetting Limited, Hong Kong
Printed by Permanent Typesetting and Printing Co., Ltd., Hong
Kong, on totally chlorine-free (TCF) paper
Cover design by Joyce C. Weston

The cover photo shows a "living machine": a symbiotic association of algae and bacteria oxygenating the waste and degrading
organic and toxic compounds.
Photo by Dann Blackwood.

UNUP-909
ISBN 92-808-0909-1
02200 P

Contents

Executive Summary

Business activities are responsible, directly or indirectly, for most human impacts on the earth's ecosystems – and business operations today are conducted with too little thought as to their sustainability – that is, the satisfying of our own needs without diminishing the chances of future generations. The term "sustainability," which has both ecological and social components, poses business an inescapable challenge: without sustainability there will soon be no more profits. Hence, business people have a strong self-interest in minimizing the ecological damage of their operations.

In this book, business people, economists, ecologists, and other thinkers outline new practical approaches that business and society, including media and educators, must take to move towards sustainability.

As José Lutzenberger, a Brazilian agronomist active in reducing toxics usage writes, much of the driving force for change in business comes from outside—in particular, from the teeming nongovernmental organizations that marshal ecological and political expertise, educate the public, bring political pressure to bear on government, and outline new and often profitable possibilities for business. But executives must take responsibility themselves for reeducating themselves and their managers. Thus Kris McDivitt, former CEO of the premier outdoor-clothing company Patagonia, tells of her self-education experiences, while Oscar Motomura, whose company runs management education programs in large Brazilian companies, describes his strategies for sensitizing and informing managers. The information needed both within companies and outside is becoming steadily fuller, and Charles Fombrun, Luis Martins, and Alice Tepper Marlin describe the work of services and groups that assess and help to improve the environonmental performance of a wide range of large corporations.

Social change takes place within the interplay among media, corporations, and the public, and Eric Utne, publisher of the innovative *Utne*

Reader, describes some of the new patterns that are emerging in America. Government also enters the picture on many levels. Monika Griefahn, Minister of the Environment in the German state of Lower Saxony, describes many types of leverage that government can exert to reduce environmental impacts and motivate companies to redesign products and processes. Herman Daly, the world-renowned economist formerly with the World Bank, outlines how ecologically based tax reforms can stop rewarding intensive resource use, pollution, and job destruction, and reward companies that produce true "goods" instead of ecological "bads."

Within the financial world, also, new ideas are stirring. Woody Tasch and Stephen Viederman, foundation executives, explain how narrow traditional notions of fiduciary responsibility among investment people are expanding to include ecological responsibility and a longer-term analysis of financial returns.

Technology, which many take to be hostile to the environment, also has a new role to play in moving toward sustainability. Gunter Pauli describes the coming zero-emissions industrial clusters, where everything we now consider "waste" becomes the raw material for an adjacent industry, greatly minimizing industry impacts on the earth. And John and Nancy Jack Todd tell of their "living machines" – complex multi-species configurations that serve human purposes while also constituting sustainable organisms.

Finally, Yvon Chouinard, founder of Patagonia, tells how he guided his highly profitable company toward limited growth, greatly reduced environmental impacts, and consistent support for positive social and ecological goals.

Fritjof Capra is the author of *The Tao of Physics, The Turning Point*, and the script for the film *Mindwalk*. His work focuses on the paradigm shift needed to remedy the crises of perception that today make it difficult to see our way toward a sustainable future. Founder and president of the Elmwood Institute in Berkeley, California, he is also co-author of *EcoManagement: The Elmwood Guide to Ecological Auditing and Sustainable Business*.

Gunter Pauli trained as an economist, obtained an MBA, and has established numerous companies. During the 1980s he undertook major research on the rising service sectors of the world economy. In 1992 he was instrumental in the building of the world's first zero-emissions factory – a Belgian detergents plant. He is now establishing the zero-emissions research program at the United Nations University in Tokyo.

Preface

Over the past fifteen years, the concept of ecological sustainability has become one of the most important guiding principles for the global ecology movement. Introduced by Lester Brown in 1981 as the challenge to satisfy our needs without diminishing the chances of future generations, and promoted ever since in the Worldwatch Institute's annual reports, *State of the World*, the concept was coupled with that of development in 1987 in the UN report of the World Commission on Environment and Development (Brundtland Report). For some, the new term "sustainable development" was simply a strategy for sustaining previous patterns of development, but most people saw it as the first official attempt to integrate the desire for development with concern for the environment.

Over the following years, the idea of sustainability continued to gain wider and wider recognition, and in 1992 it was brought to the attention of millions around the world during the UN Conference on Environment and Development in Rio de Janeiro, popularly known as the "Earth Summit." The Earth Summit was a follow-up to the UN Conference on the Human Environment, held in Stockholm twenty years earlier, which had made "the environment" an issue on the international political agenda. The attendance of the Earth Summit and the parallel non-governmental events in Rio by 35,000 people, including over a hundred heads of state, was a powerful testimony to the dramatic increase of environmental awareness during the twenty years between those two UN conferences. The number of journalists in Rio alone exceeded the total number of participants in Stockholm.

The Earth Summit marked the beginning of a new era, dominated no longer by the East-West conflict but by concern for ecological sustainability, a concern that transcends all differences of race, culture, ideology, or class. As editors of this book, we come from very different fields – Fritjof from science and Gunter from business – but we share this deep concern about how to create a sustainable future for our children and all coming generations.

We have often imagined a new sustainable world, and at times we have encountered a strong resonance in the business community. But more often we seemed to speak a different language, sometimes even to live in a different world. How, then, we asked ourselves, can we help to steer business toward sustainability without being dictatorial, without trying to impose our logic? We feel very strongly that the time has come to take the initiative and present in a compact, readable book the key factors that can motivate executives to change course. This is why we have teamed up to edit the present book for the United Nations University.

This volume offers a rich dialogue of many voices, for which we have tried to provide some context in editorial comments at the beginning of each chapter (in italics). In addition, we have added our recommendations of essential readings for executives in the Appendix.

We are grateful to all the distinguished contributors to this volume. They are extremely busy people, but they found the time to write the informed and insightful chapters that follow.

We are also grateful to Ernest Callenbach who served as textual editor for the volume, skillfully helping our international band of contributors toward the standard of world English that is, increasingly, the lingua franca of business as well as science and other fields.

Our special thanks go to Trena Cleland who was essential in the complex task of processing manuscripts that came in electronically in many different forms, and also assisted in copy editing. Without her expertise and untiring help under great time pressure we could never have met our deadline.

We are also grateful to the Center for Ecoliteracy, formerly the Elmwood Institute, for hosting the editorial part of this project.

Last but not least, it is our pleasure to thank the United Nations University for sponsoring this venture. We feel that the UNU is an ideal forum for this dialogue. The UN has repeatedly taken the lead in bringing the need for ecological sustainability to the world's attention, and the UN University, according to its charter, serves as a center for ideas and a platform for creativity. In the framework of the

UNU Agenda 21, several innovative programs have been launched, including a search for eco-restructuring, a new design for industry, and a zero-emissions research initiative, based on clustering industries, which is discussed below in Chapter 10. The UNU is also undertaking a book series in which this volume is the first publication, and there are plans to complement the book with a CD-ROM bringing new forms of education to our readers.

It is thus most fitting that this dialogue on how to steer business toward sustainability should be published under the auspices of the United Nations in the year of its fiftieth anniversary. The Earth is our common home and creating a sustainable world for our children and all future generations is our common task.

Fritjof Capra and Gunter Pauli
Berkeley and Tokyo, January 1995

Introduction

1

The Challenge

Fritjof Capra and Gunter Pauli

As the century draws to a close, environmental concerns have become of paramount importance. The survival of humanity and of the planet are at stake. Concern about the environment is no longer one of many "single issues"; it is the *context* of everything else – of our lives, our business, our politics.

Today we are faced with a whole series of global problems which are harming the biosphere and human life in alarming ways that may soon become irreversible. We have ample documentation about the extent and significance of these problems. One of the best recent accounts is the book *The Ecology of Commerce* by Paul Hawken, which discusses the central role of business in global environmental destruction and, at the same time, the unique opportunity for business to become the driving force of ecological restoration. After a thorough review of the series of ecological catastrophes we face, Hawken reaches a devastating conclusion:

Quite simply, our business practices are destroying life on earth. Given current corporate practices, not one wildlife reserve, wilderness, or indigenous culture will survive the global market economy. We know that every living natural system on the planet is disintegrating before our eyes. The land, water, air and sea have been functionally transformed from life-giving systems into repositories for waste. There is no polite way to say that business is ravaging the world.[1]

The great challenge of our time is to create sustainable forms of business, embedded in sustainable communities. Lester Brown of the

[1] Paul Hawken, *The Ecology of Commerce*, Harper Collins, New York, 1993; p. 3.

Worldwatch Institute, who has been one of the main advocates of ecological sustainability for many years, defines a sustainable society as one that is able to satisfy its needs without diminishing the chances of future generations.[2]

How can we deal with this tremendous challenge? Where do we start?

The more we study the major problems of our time, the more we come to realize that they cannot be understood in isolation. They are systemic problems – interconnected and interdependent. Stabilizing world population will only be possible when poverty is reduced world-wide. The extinction of animal and plant species on a massive scale will continue as long as the South is burdened by massive debts. Only if we stop the international arms trade will we have the resources to prevent the many destructive impacts on the biosphere and on human life.

In fact, the more we study the situation, the more we realize that, ultimately, these problems are just different facets of one single crisis, which is essentially a crisis of perception. It derives from the fact that most of us, and especially our large social institutions, subscribe to the concepts of an outdated world view, a perception of reality inadequate for dealing with our overpopulated, globally interconnected world.

At the same time, researchers at the leading edge of science, various social movements, and numerous alternative networks are developing a new vision of reality that will form the basis of our future technologies, economic systems, and social institutions. So we are at the beginning of a fundamental change of world view in science and society, a change of "paradigms" as radical as the Copernican Revolution.

The paradigm that is now receding has dominated Western industrial culture for several hundred years, during which it has shaped modern society and has significantly influenced all parts of the world. This paradigm consists of a number of ideas and values, among them the view of the universe as a mechanical system composed of elementary building blocks, the view of the human body as a machine, the view of life in society as a competitive struggle for existence, the belief in unlimited material progress to be achieved through economic and technological growth, and – last, not least – the belief that a society in which the female is everywhere subsumed under the male is one that follows a basic law of nature. All of these assumptions

[2] Lester R. Brown, *Building a Sustainable Society*, Norton, New York, 1981.

2

have been fatefully challenged by recent events. And, indeed, a radical revision of them is now occurring.

The new paradigm may be called a holistic world view, seeing the world as an integrated whole rather than a dissociated collection of parts. It may also be called an ecological view, if the term "ecological" is used in a much broader and deeper sense than usual. This broader and deeper sense of "ecological" is associated with a specific philosophical school and, moreover, with a global grassroots movement, known as "deep ecology," which is rapidly gaining prominence. The philosophical school was founded by the Norwegian philosopher Arne Naess in the early seventies with his distinction between "shallow" and "deep" ecology. This distinction is now widely accepted as a very useful terminology for referring to a major division within contemporary environmental thought.

Shallow ecology is anthropocentric. It views humans as above, or outside of nature, as the source of all value, and ascribes only instrumental, or use value to nature. Deep ecology does not separate humans from the natural environment, nor does it separate anything else from it. It does not see the world as a collection of isolated objects but rather as a network of phenomena that are fundamentally interconnected and interdependent. Deep ecology recognizes the intrinsic values of all living beings and views humans as just one particular strand in the web of life. It recognizes that we are all embedded in, and dependent upon, the cyclical processes of nature.

Ultimately, deep ecological awareness is spiritual or religious awareness. When the concept of the human spirit is understood as the mode of consciousness in which the individual feels connected to the cosmos as a whole, it becomes clear that ecological awareness is spiritual in its deepest essence. It is therefore not surprising that the emerging new vision of reality, based on deep ecological awareness, is consistent with the so-called "perennial philosophy" of spiritual traditions, whether we talk about the spirituality of Christian mystics, that of Buddhists, or the philosophy and cosmology underlying the American Indian traditions.

In science, the theory of living systems provides the most appropriate scientific formulation of deep ecology. It is a theory that is only now fully emerging but has its roots in several scientific fields that were developed during the first half of the century – organismic biology, gestalt psychology, ecology, general systems theory, and cybernetics. In all these fields scientists explored living systems, i.e. integrated wholes whose properties cannot be reduced to those of smaller parts.

3

Living systems include individual organisms, parts of organisms, and communities of organisms, such as social systems and ecosystems. All these are irreducible wholes whose specific structures arise from the interactions and interdependence of their parts. Systems theory tells us that all these living systems share a set of common properties and principles of organization.

In our attempts to build and nurture sustainable communities we can learn valuable lessons from ecosystems, because ecosystems *are* sustainable communities of plants, animals, and microorganisms. To understand these lessons, we need to learn nature's language. We need to become ecologically literate. Indeed, one of the main reasons we are destroying our natural environment is our ecological illiteracy, our ignorance of the principles of ecology. It is a sobering thought that the average adult in the industrialized world can recognize one thousand brand names and logos but fewer than ten local plants.

Being ecologically literate means understanding how ecosystems organize themselves so as to maximize sustainability. This is the lesson we have to learn to build sustainable human communities. We need to revitalize our communities – including our educational communities, business communities, and political communities – so that the basic principles of ecology become manifest in them as principles of education, management, and politics. Today, this is especially important for business, which has been designed without any attention to the basic principles of ecology. As Paul Hawken puts it, "what is good for business is almost always bad for nature."[3]

The first principle of ecology is interdependence. All members of an ecosystem are interconnected in a vast and intricate network of relationships, the web of life. They derive their essential properties and, in fact, their very existence from their relationships to other things. Interdependence is the nature of all ecological relationships. The success of the whole system depends on the success of its individual members, while the success of each member depends upon the success of the system as a whole.

The principle of interdependence implies a shift of perception from objects to relationships. In business this includes, among other things, a shift from products to services. For example, the managers of a car company should say: We are not in the business of selling cars; we are in the business of providing mobility. This will include cars, but also trains, bicycles, buses, and – above all – integrated systems of these

[3] Paul Hawken, op. cit., p. 57.

4

means of transportation. Similarly, the managers of an oil company should say: We are not in the business of selling oil; we are in the business of satisfying our customers' energy needs. The path to sustainable business begins with this focus on relationships, rather than objects or products.

Another important principle of ecology is the cyclical nature of most ecological processes. The interactions among the members of an ecosystem involve the exchange of energy and resources in continual cycles – the water cycle, the CO_2 cycle and the various nutrient cycles. Communities of organisms have evolved over billions of years, continually using and recycling the same molecules of minerals, water, and air.

The lesson for business here is obvious. The present clash between business and nature, between economics and ecology, is mainly due to the fact that nature is cyclical, whereas our industrial systems are linear, taking up energy and resources from the earth, transforming them into products plus waste, discarding the waste, and finally throwing away the products also after they have been used. Sustainable patterns of production and consumption need to be cyclical, imitating the processes in ecosystems.[4] To achieve such cyclical patterns, we need to fundamentally redesign our businesses and our economy. Such a redesign of business organizations is currently under way in Sweden, where an eminent cancer researcher, Karl-Henrik Robért, has unified the country in moving from linear to cyclical processes in a remarkable nation-wide program, called "The Natural Step."[5]

Solar energy drives all ecological cycles, and green plants play a vital role in this flow of energy. In the marvelous process of photosynthesis, solar energy is converted into chemical energy and bound in organic substances, while oxygen is released to renew the air. Again, the lesson for business is obvious. Solar energy in its many forms is the only kind of energy that is sustainable and economically efficient (if we count the costs of energy production honestly!). By disregarding this principle of ecology, our political and corporate leaders again and again endanger the health and well-being of millions around the world.

As the nutrients and other resources are passed along through an ecosystem, the organisms along the ecological cycles are engaged in

[4] See ibid., pp. 62ff.
[5] See Karl-Henrik Robért, "Educating a Nation: The Natural Step," *In Context*, No. 28.

various forms of cooperation. In the nineteenth century, the Social Darwinists saw only competition in nature. Today we know that all competition takes place within a broader context of cooperation involving countless forms of partnership. Indeed, partnership – the tendency to associate, establish links, live inside one another and co-operate – is an essential characteristic of living organisms.

A sustainable business organization will apply this principle to cooperation and partnership along product cycles and in countless other ways, both internally within the company and industry-wide. Here we encounter again the basic tension between economics and ecology that we need to overcome. Economics deals with quantity, competition, expansion; ecology deals with quality, cooperation, conservation.

Principles of Ecology

INTERDEPENDENCE
All members of an ecosystem are interconnected in a web of relationships, in which all life processes depend on one another.

ECOLOGICAL CYCLES
The interdependencies among the members of an ecosystem involve the exchange of energy and resources in continual cycles.

ENERGY FLOW
Solar energy, transformed into chemical energy by the photosynthesis of green plants, drives all ecological cycles.

PARTNERSHIP
All living members of an ecosystem are engaged in a subtle interplay of competition and cooperation, involving countless forms of partnership.

FLEXIBILITY
Ecological cycles have the tendency to maintain themselves in a flexible state, characterized by interdependent fluctuations of their variables.

DIVERSITY
The stability of an ecosystem depends on the degree of complexity of its network of relationships; in other words, on the diversity of the ecosystem.

COEVOLUTION
Most species in an ecosystem coevolve through an interplay of creation and mutual adaptation.

SUSTAINABILITY
The long-term survival of each species in an ecosystem depends on a limited resource base. Ecosystems organize themselves according to the principles summarized above so as to maximize sustainability.

The general shift from domination to partnership is an essential part of the shift from the mechanistic to the ecological paradigm. Whereas a machine is properly understood through domination and control, the understanding of a living system will be much more successful if approached through cooperation and partnership. Cooperative relationships are an essential characteristic of life.

The principles of ecology mentioned so far – interdependence, the cyclical flows of energy and resources, cooperation, and partnership – are all different aspects of the same pattern of organization. This is how ecosystems organize themselves to maximize sustainability. Once we have understood this pattern of organization, we can ask more detailed questions. For example, what is the resilience of these ecological communities? How do they react to outside disturbances? How do they develop and evolve? These questions lead us to three further principles of ecology – flexibility, diversity, and coevolution.

Flexibility is manifest in the fact that the network structure of an ecosystem is not rigid but is constantly fluctuating. When changing environmental conditions, e.g., an unusually warm summer, disturb one link in an ecological cycle, the entire cycle acts as a self-regulating feedback loop and soon brings the situation back into balance. And since these environmental disturbances happen all the time, the variables in an ecological cycle (nutrient supplies, population densities, etc.) undergo continual interdependent fluctuations. These fluctuations represent the ecosystem's flexibility. The more variables are kept fluctuating, the more dynamic is the system, the greater its flexibility, the greater its ability to adapt to changing environmental conditions.

All ecological cycles are feedback loops that have the tendency to maintain themselves in a flexible state, characterized by continual fluctuations of their variables. When changing environmental conditions disturb one link in an ecological cycle, the entire cycle acts as a self-regulating feedback loop and soon brings the situation back into balance. And since these disturbances happen all the time, the variables in an ecological cycle fluctuate continually.

These fluctuations represent the ecosystem's flexibility. Lack of flexibility manifests itself as stress. In particular, stress will occur when one or more variables of the system are pushed to their extreme values, which induces increased rigidity throughout the system. Temporary stress is an essential aspect of life, but prolonged stress is harmful and destructive to the system. These considerations lead to the important realization that managing a business organization means to find the *optimal* values for the systems variables. If one tries to maximize any single variable instead of optimizing it, this will invariably lead to the destruction of the system as a whole.

In ecosystems, this flexibility through fluctuations does not always work, because there can be very severe disturbances that actually wipe out an entire species. In other words, one of the links in the ecosystem's network is destroyed. An ecological community will be resilient when this link is not the only one of its kind; when there are other connections that can at least partially fulfill its functions. In other words, the more complex the network, the greater the diversity of its interconnections, the more resilient it will be. The same is true in human communities. Diversity means many different relationships, many different approaches to the same problem. A diverse community is a resilient community, capable of adapting easily to changing situations.

The loss of biodiversity, i.e. the daily loss of species, is in the long run one of our most severe global environmental problems. And because of the close integration of tribal indigenous people into their ecosystems, the loss of biodiversity is closely tied to the loss of cultural diversity, the extinction of traditional tribal cultures. This is especially important today. As the beliefs and practices of the industrial culture are being recognized as part of the global ecological crisis, there is an urgent need for a wider understanding of cultural patterns that are sustainable. The vast folk wisdom of American Indian, African, and Asian traditions has been viewed as inferior and backward by the industrial culture. It is time to reverse this Euro-centric arrogance and to recognize that many of these traditions – their ways of knowing, technologies, knowledge of foods and medicines, forms of aesthetic expression, patterns of social interaction, communal relationships, etc. – embody the ecological wisdom we so urgently need today.

Finally, let us turn to the time dimension of ecosystems. All living systems develop, and all development is learning. Therefore, a sustainable community is always a learning community – a community which continually changes, develops, and learns. At the level of species, development and learning manifest as the creative unfolding of life in the process of evolution. In an ecosystem, evolution is not limited to the gradual adaptation of organisms to their environment, because the environment is itself a network of living systems capable of adaptation and creativity. Organisms and environment adapt to one another – they coevolve. All forms of life on Earth have coevolved in this way as integral components of ecosystems for billions of years.

8

Coevolution combines the principle of partnership with the dynamic of change and development. Again, there is a lesson to be learned for business. As business partnerships evolve, each partner better understands the needs of the other. In a true, committed partnership both partners learn and change – they coevolve.

These, then, are the basic principles of ecology – interdependence, recycling, the energy flow from the sun, partnership, flexibility, diversity, coevolution, and, as a consequence of all those, sustainability. As we go toward the beginning of a new millennium, the survival of humanity will depend on our ecological literacy, on our ability to understand these principles of ecology and live accordingly. (F.C.)

Sometimes it seems that it is not merely the environment that is at stake. If business does not change its strategy, business itself may very well be at stake. Many – if not most – consider industry as part of the problem. But many others realize that business is the solution. We believe that if the corporate world does not play an active role in redefining its own operations, moving toward sustainability, the world as a whole will never succeed in that task.

But, on the other hand, business alone cannot overcome the present challenges. The time has come to establish solid cooperation among policy-makers, scientists, opinion leaders, the community, and business. And it is up to business executives to take a pro-active role in the definition of business's new agenda and the priorities it must share with the community. They know by now all too well that if the setting of the agenda is left to other players in society, business cannot get down to business.

Executives know too that doing more business the same way as in the past is a guarantee of failure. By the same token, the time is past when scholars, governments, or environmental organizations could hand down a doctrine from some high pulpit of academic certainty or from emotional distress and fears. Rather, cooperation among all those who have a stake in the future of society is critical.

The objective of defining strategies to steer business toward sustainability is *not* to invent new technologies. Much technology is really not new knowledge; it is, as Peter Drucker has said, "putting together things that no one had thought of putting together before." The reserve of untapped technological breakthroughs, either to be reinvented because we have neglected them or to be discovered because we have not bothered to study the great genius of Nature, must be brought into play, and the faster the better.

The days of the notion of "competitive edge" are numbered.

Business will have to convert its strategic approach to the development of a "sustainable advantage." Traditional economic theory prescribes that the competitive edge of a company depends on the efficient combination of capital, raw materials, and labor. Over the past decades, economists have expanded this to the importance of technology and information.

Companies in crisis wonder how to improve their competitive edge. This was relevant in the sixties, it is relevant today, and it will be relevant in the 21st century. But while the questions remain the same, the answers change. In the sixties, when a corporation felt the pinch from its competitors and looked for a solution, the president was told to stop trying to just *sell* his products – he needed a marketing strategy. The need to listen to the clients' wishes and preferences was the first sign that we were operating in a market characterized by over-supply. If someone were not to adapt to the customer, he would be eliminated. It was the era of Philip Kotler and the "four P's." There is no company today that questions the importance of marketing.

In the early seventies, when the first oil crisis devastated industry, the key question was how to regain a competitive position at a time when increased energy costs affected pricing and caused high inflation, undermining consumer confidence. The answer at the time was *productivity*. There was no doubt that those who could produce more with the same level of input in terms of raw materials, capital, or labor, were to win. It was the first time that Japanese industry was called in to serve as an example. Indeed, the Japanese overcame the first oil crisis faster than anyone else and integrated more robots and information technology, catapulting their production industries to the forefront of worldwide competition.

In the late seventies, the second oil crisis hit the West. Again, industries that lost market share searched for a renaissance of their businesses, and *quality* was identified as the cutting-edge factor that could enable a company to out-compete anyone in the market. It was the time of quality control circles and total quality management. Indeed, as the American management gurus Juran and Deming professed from Japan, bad quality is a cost and good quality leads to a leaner cost structure and higher customer loyalty.

In the early eighties, Western industry again faced decreasing market shares. After having invested massively in quality and productivity programs, it became obvious that more was needed to succeed long-term in the world competitive game. The concept of *just-in-*

time was advanced as the next avenue to success. The Japanese were supposed to have implemented the *kan-ban* system first and foremost, and the West was advised to learn from the Land of the Rising Sun once again. It generated a third wave of industrial tourism.

In the late eighties *service* was presented as the next panacea for success. American corporations embarked on drastic outsourcing, giving rise to a most successful service industry, which is basically the result of shifting people from in-house service providers to outside, cutting employment on industry's payroll and boosting the "success" of services. It became clear that up to 75 percent of the value added created by industry were services to production. The Swatch was a prime example. It didn't matter if the successful watches of the seventies were made in Taiwan or Macao. Labor costs represent only three percent of the total value added involved in a sale and as a result, it is possible to pay considerably more, as it does not significantly affect the end price to the customer. Low labor costs did not matter anymore; they were replaced in the North by "no labor costs." The design factor and communication skills represented the real service to the customer.

In the early nineties, when industry was desperately searching for new ideas on how to compete, again a new theory was advanced: re-engineering was the message promoted by the management guru Hammer. The message is simple: start all over again, and start from scratch! And, if someone is not willing to follow, "break a few legs."

Today, companies are expected to excel simultaneously in all six elements: marketing, productivity, quality, just-in-time, services, and re-engineering. Performance in each of these areas is considered a precondition for successful entry into the market. If a business integrates all these elements, then it will have the right to be in the market. If a company wishes to outperform the average businesses, if it is out to gain market share, more will be needed.

What more can be offered? In order to address this effectively, we have to leave supply-side management and study trends in demand. Actually, we are returning to the stage of marketing, to listening to what the customer really wants.

Over the past five years, consumers have enjoyed low levels of inflation. The market wants "more for less." This means that companies have to cut costs even further and offer more. The continuous drive toward better perceived value for less money is difficult to achieve today because we are at a time when business cannot hide increased value through price hikes, or hide increasing costs behind inflation. Today, something more is needed to perform well, to do better in the game. But what is it?

At present, economists cannot agree on any single issue that is to dominate. However, on the basis of thorough market analyses in Europe, Japan, and the U.S., it has been concluded that during the next few years, ethical standards, a moral commitment, and high environmental performance will not only become an integral part of the corporate strategy; these will become the way to outperform the industry and reestablish that unique marketing position so badly desired. It will be the only way to develop a sustainable advantage.

Today, more than 40 percent of consumers in the U.S. indicate that when the same price and quality are being offered, moral, ethical, and environmental issues considered important by the consumers will determine their choices. Of course, there is a very broad variety of themes that companies can address: biodiversity, AIDS, animal testing, minority rights, Third World development, fair trade, healthy and organic farming, and so on.

Several companies have succeeded in setting an ethical or moral agenda and appealing to a large share of the market. These are concerns that attract the community and have to form an integral part of corporate behavior if business is to deserve long-term respect in society. What is most interesting is that consumers are increasingly well-informed and capable of seeing through marketing slogans that are not based on genuine commitment.

This does not imply that all companies today are unethical, immoral, or unconcerned with the environment. But companies will have to be thoroughly committed to doing more for society than merely playing a role in generating value added and creating profits for their shareholders. The company of the 21st century will have different responsibilities to assume in society from those generally expected today.

It is dramatic to note, for example, that on environmental issues not even ten percent of the public believes statements made by companies. In a recent survey in Europe, environmental volunteer organizations were identified as the most credible sources of information. This implies that if business does not take a proactive and really credible leap towards converting its operations on the basis of the concept of ecological sustainability, it will lose its legitimacy.

At the time when companies have to re-engineer their operations, it is timely to take the next step forward and retool the company, integrating the most rigid moral, ethical, and ecological standards. A company is a most efficiently organized structure, the only type in society that creates value added based on the principle of minimum input and maximum output. At a time when governments and NGOs are searching for more efficient modes of operation, business practice is welcome indeed. And, if ethical, moral, and environmental considerations are combined with the other cutting-edge factors, this will be a formidable force indeed.

The biggest weakness of industrial conglomerates today is that they have embarked during the last 20 years on programs to cut costs and remain competitive without taking considerations of the community and the limits of nature into account. Companies only looked at (1) cutting employees and (2) generating more money with less cash.

Productivity increases were first equated with a reduction in personnel. As the president of the Taco Bell restaurant chain remarked, "The ideal company is one where I work on my own with my 10,000 franchisees." All other people are to be considered potentially redundant. This is not exactly the bright picture of the future that communities project for themselves.

The logging communities in the Pacific Northwest have not heard of job creation for decades. The only story they have heard is that it is necessary to cut employment to save the other few jobs that are left. This strategy of business has generated a major weakness. Proctor & Gamble, IBM, and Chrysler have embarked on major cost reduction programs, cutting tens of thousands of job and closing dozens of factories. The support these companies have built up in their communities is fundamentally based on the provision of local jobs. The systematic loss of employment erodes the basis of trust on which business became established in the community. Whereas no one debates the need for an efficient organization, the narrow focus on people as the only one of the three critical input factors (people, capital, and raw materials) to bear the brunt of higher productivity is an anomaly.

The second drive toward cutting costs and improving returns is to seek more return for less cash. Corporations desire to maintain their financial performance and to continuously improve the return on their investment. The just-in-time program frees up a lot of cash previously locked up in raw materials, supplies, half-fabricated goods, and finished products.

"Tax technologies" were introduced, making use of tax havens through complicated holding structures spanning the world, with the objective that companies pay the least amount of taxes to the communities in which they operate. New investment commitments were made subject to bargaining over tax rebates and even straightforward subsidies.

How can a company that does everything to evade taxes – making use of the loopholes in the international laws, soliciting major subsidies, and cutting jobs – ever expect a relationship of trust with society? No loyalty will be generated through this type of behavior, certainly not loyalty sustainable for business over time.

While industry has rightfully been searching for productivity in labor and in capital, it has never sought with the same vigor a dramatically improved level of productivity in the use of virgin raw materials. If industry decreased warehousing of input factors from three months to fifteen minutes – as is the case in the automobile industry – why can't we imagine industry reducing the need for virgin materials by 90 percent? The redesign of the warehousing systems and delivery systems took less than five years. So, is it unreasonable to expect that industry will eliminate several of its waste streams in a few years' time and reduce the intake of virgin materials by 90 percent by the end of the century? It is urgent!

Industry will endanger its own future if it does *not* take this route. Industry can reinforce its critical role in society by firmly engaging in massive materials reduction with the same zest as productivity of labor was increased, quality was improved, and just-in-time was established. If in addition business succeeds in integrating moral, ethical, and environmental issues in its strategic approach, then it will become a formidable, respected, and sustainable presence in harmony with the community and the Earth. The companies which achieve this will be the winners, while those which neglect it will be the dinosaurs of tomorrow.

(G.P.)

2

NGOs as a Driving Force

José A. Lutzenberger

In companies, as in other human organizations, powerful tendencies toward inertia and maintenance of the status quo mean that change is usually driven either by competitive pressures or profit-seeking. Moreover, in industrial societies business usually has effective control over most actions of government. The result is that the movement toward sustainability has to be driven mainly by citizens, who have learned to mobilize themselves in so-called "NGOs" – non-governmental organizations. Business needs to see this "other" perspective, and therefore our dialogue begins with this point of view.

NGOs have concerns for health and safety of individuals and communities, environmental protection, political responsiveness, and many other areas, and they have proliferated immensely in most countries of the world. They pressure governments to take new actions and reform traditional practices; they attempt to use the power of media and public opinion to influence companies directly; and they educate the public about issues, so that citizens can exert pressure directly upon companies – either through changed consumer behavior or publicly visible demonstrations and other actions.

José Lutzenberger is an agronomist and engineer from the Brazilian state of Rio Grande do Sul who spent many years working for the large chemical company BASF but then quit his job and began a vigorous and successful campaign against the activities of the agrochemical industry. Lutzenberger served as Brazil's Minister of the Environment from 1990 to 1992 and is today one of the best known environmentalists in the Southern Hemisphere.

In spite of his high profile as an environmental activist, Lutzen-

berger is also a successful businessman who knows how to cooperate with large companies and change them from within. For example, he fought Riocell, a large cellulose and paper factory in southern Brazil, for many years because of the way it polluted the environment, but during those years he always remained on speaking terms with the factory's director. Eventually, the director ended up hiring Lutzenberger as a consultant – with dramatic results. Before Lutzenberger's involvement with the company, Riocell spent half a million dollars a year burying its (mostly organic) waste in huge pits, which polluted and devastated the environment. Now, the factory hands over its total waste to Lutzenberger's waste management company, where it is processed, turned into fertilizer and other products for organic farming, and sold to a network of organic farmers. As a result, the environmental degradation has stopped, the factory saves half a million dollars a year, and 99.6% of the waste is sold. The waste processing involves low technology and thus is labor intensive, supporting 50 full-time jobs.

In addition to his waste management company, Lutzenberger also runs a landscaping company. He created a park right on the Riocell factory site. Instead of waste dumps, there are now fish ponds and reeds with an abundance of birds. The whole park, situated on a big delta, is a thriving ecosystem, wrapped right around the factory. Thus at Riocell, ecological sustainability has become an industrial achievement.

In this chapter, Lutzenberger shares his reflections on years of environmental activism, reviewing the process by which NGOs he has been associated with have attempted to reduce Brazil's use of agricultural toxics. The story illustrates both the energy and tenacity that NGOs bring to their task and the resourcefulness with which industries fight back.

We believe that people like José Lutzenberger and the NGOs they represent are like antennae in our society, reflecting the mood and spirit of the time before ordinary people can see it. In previous centuries, artists have often served as such sensitive antennae. Perhaps the NGOs of the environmental movement in our time should be considered equivalent to the Michelangelos, Beethovens, and Van Goghs of previous eras.

I became an environmentalist out of despair. As a student in agronomy in the late 1940s I often spent my vacations surveying paddy-rice fields, measuring the crop size for the bank that financed the planters. Our rice fields are artificial swamps of a sort and most of them were and often still are contiguous to natural wetlands, the majority of which were mostly intact. This gave me a chance to enjoy intensive observation of South American waterfowl, from plover, ibis, and ducks to egret, crane, cormorant, and spoonbill. There were various species of storks as well as the stately taja, a giant plover the size of a turkey, and all the smaller birds that lived in and around the water or on the fields and in the woods. From early childhood I had always been a naturalist, so these were some of the happiest times of my life. Our climate in Rio Grande do Sul is subtropical, but most of the birds are the same that live in the Pantanal, which is tropical. Some of them even migrate between our region all the way south to Patagonia and through the Pantanal to Amazonia. Among the swallows that hunt insects by flying so low they almost scrape the water, some are known to go as far as North America. Then there was the capibara, the largest rodent in the world, the nutria, and sometimes we could even observe one of the most graceful and playful creatures I know, the otter. Everything was intact; most of the landscape was pristine. Farming was still what we today would call organic farming. But nobody used this term and the word ecology was yet unknown.

Some twenty years later, after having lived and worked in other countries, I came back to my home state in Southern Brazil. I then did a lot of travelling and saw most of the rice growing regions again. I was shocked, horrified! The birds had been decimated almost to extinction. Intensive and ruthless use of agri-poisons, not only in the rice plantations but on all crops, was causing more damage than uncontrolled hunting and partial obliteration of habitats had ever done before. In some cases it was so bad that big rice planters would invite hunters to hunt out everything they could before the application of the first poison, with the argument that it would all die anyway. At the time a terrible herbicide was in use. It was applied into the water, dripped from drums mounted over the entry canal of the paddy. It killed all life in the water and hence everything that fed on it.

I'm the kind of person who, when confronted with something bad that could be changed for the better, will get a very bad conscience if I do not act. Fortunately this attitude is not too rare yet or the world would not be teeming with NGOs. I've worked as a government official, and government can do useful things – if it is prodded enough. But the impetus comes from the NGOs of the world, as our Brazilian story makes clear.

I talked to my colleagues, the agronomists. Most of them did not care, but some did. We then campaigned for a law that would make it a requirement for farmers, when buying their poisons, to present a prescription signed by an agronomist. The agronomist would be responsible and liable in case of damage.

Most of the poisons were used preventively. In the case of insecticides the farmers would spray as soon as they saw any insect whatever, even lady beetles. People are so alienated from nature today they often cannot distinguish a spider from an insect. The chemical industry even proposed "spraying calendars." The spraying was against pests that *could* appear at the respective time, not only against what really constituted a threat. The poisons were cheap, and credit was subsidized.

A couple of years later, campaigning within the associations of Brazilian agronomists who worked at the county, state, and federal levels, we obtained a majority for prescription. We then asked for one more step. To avoid conflict of interest, only agronomists not working for the chemical industry should be eligible for writing prescriptions, for the same reason a pharmacist should not prescribe what he sells. This provoked a lot more opposition, as too many agronomists made their living selling or promoting agri-chemicals. A few more years and we won. The Ministry of Agriculture always fiercely opposed any idea of prescription, but we got the semi-official bank that had the monopoly for agricultural credits to accept it as a policy for granting them.

This rapidly led to a considerable reduction in the sales and use of poisons. Previously it had also been the policy of the bank to require that a sizable portion of the credit money go into pesticides, whether needed or not. It is easy to imagine who suggested this to them. Agronomists also became more careful; many even looked into books on toxicology. Some developed methods of appraising whether pest attack was economically significant or not, suggesting chemical warfare only when serious reductions in yield were to be expected. More often than not the cost of the damage caused by some bug or fungus is much lower than the cost of the poison. Many farmers learned to recognize their pests better and realized they could save money by spending less on unnecessary inputs.

Initially it was only the regional office of the bank that imposed prescriptions but, then, by lucky chance, the president in the national head-office applied the new policy to the whole country. That was decidedly too much for the Ministry. It suddenly issued a decree that also instituted prescription, but with somewhat different provisions. Where we excluded agronomists working for the chemical industry, they allowed all of them, whether self-employed, employed by farmers or working for the government, and including those who were in industry to sign the prescriptions. There was another important addition. We made no distinction among poisons concerning toxicological classification. Prescription applied to everything, but the Ministry now limited it to only those pesticides in toxicological classes I and II, the most toxic and persistent. Classifications III and IV, which then included relatively harmless substances such as sulfur, were free.

Well, it was still progress compared to the initial situation, where any small boy could go to the farmers' supply shop and freely buy extremely toxic and/or persistent poisons, without even being asked what he was going to do with them. Brazil also had a world-class toxicological classification for agricultural biocides. So we were not too unhappy.

Then something interesting happened. The Ministry of Health issued a new classification. Now all the really bad stuff that was on the market in Brazil and that had been classified I and II was shifted to III and IV ... But the agricultural bank decided not to follow suit; they continued as before. Then, again within a very short time, another curious thing happened. The national agency controlling the banks took away their monopoly and allowed all banks to lend to farmers. Some of them reinstituted the obligation that a certain percentage of the money must go to pesticides.

So we decided to work on a different level. In our state legislature we got a majority of deputies to approve a new law that made prescription mandatory and that required state registration for all agripoisons, regardless of whether they had federal registration or not. The definition "agri-poison" (agro-tóxico) became law, as against the word used by industry, "defensivo agrìcola," which translates freely as "defensive treatment." The new law also banned chlorinated hydrocarbons and gave NGOs power of appeal in registration. In only a few days our governor, who had never shown an interest in these questions, vetoed the law. Could all this be coincidence? Incredible coincidence!

Our state constitution allows the governor's veto to be overthrown by a seventy-five per cent majority. It was unanimously overthrown. Soon, other state parliaments voted similar laws, some better than ours, which had some flaws because it had been prepared in a hurry.

Among other details we had forgotten to include the aspect of advertising that did not draw attention to the danger involved with these poisons. Sixteen states now had good legislation. These included all those where agri-poison use was intensive.

We were all very surprised at the help we got from our state deputies. I think the success was due to the fact that the issue was not raised by a green party as it would have been in Europe but by concerned citizens and NGOs, oriented by experts in the field. The leaders of the movement were all agronomists and their associations on the county, state and federal levels embraced the fight. This was in the early eighties. Today these associations are mostly back in the hands of people who follow the official line.

Brazil does not have a green party worth that name. I think this is very good. I always thought ecology must permeate all parties; it is too important to be appropriated by one group. When ecological issues are presented as the defense of life for our children and of future generations, who can openly be against it? As a party issue the story would be different.

We were very happy but it did not last long. The chemical industry went to the Supreme Court and argued that our state laws were unconstitutional. They insisted only the federal level could decide and said the Ministry of Agriculture could decide by decree.

It took the Court about a year to reach a verdict. The nine Supreme judges individually took the dossier home for study and then decided separately. After some time, four had already decided in our favor. We were sure to win. We knew the opinions of two of the other five. But then, another coincidence: three judges retired and were replaced. The industry won. I hope someday someone will tell this whole fascinating story in all its detail.

But industry did not reckon with another coincidence, this one against them and of their own making. It so happened that soon after the decision, the new Minister of Agriculture was a friend of ours, a traditional politician from our state, who had been one of our governors. Since the law now said the minister could decide by decree, he did. But one more coincidence occurred. It did not take a month before the minister was replaced. His successor had nothing more urgent to do than to revoke the decree.

This short outline of a very complicated story that is not over yet and that now goes into its third decade illustrates how difficult and frustrating it can be for environmentalists to overcome the unending ruses of the powerful. But it also shows the power of the citizen. If you are knowledgeable, have determination, and accept personal sacrifice, there is much that can be achieved. In this case, even though the industry often seemed to come out on top, something was won that they cannot destroy. There is now a new, growing consciousness in agriculture and among consumers. The use of poisons has gone down considerably. The initial aim of the industry, an eight-fold increase in sales from 1974 to 1984, was only half reached and then sales fell back to almost the initial amount.

So nature has had a chance to recover. In the case of our paddy rice the water fowl are all back, as beautiful as ever. I cannot describe the joy it gives me when every late afternoon, on Gaia-Corner, the rural center of our Foundation, I can observe enormous flocks of egrets and ibis flying to their roosting places in V-formation. A couple of cranes have taken up residence with us and cormorants dive for fish. A family of otters build their caves at our pond.

More and more younger and also older farmers, agronomists, and students come to our courses on organic rice growing and regenerative farming. Soon we will also bring here whole classes of youngsters with their teachers. We will show "how to wonder," as Rachel Carson would say, to help them see the marvels of the living world and to relate to it in a spiritual way.

Our place is especially well suited for this. When we first saw it ten years ago, it was like a big sterile crater. An enormous quarry, producing gravel for road building, had just been closed down. We had to fight a project to turn it into a garbage dump for the nearby city. Then the big hole filled with water. It is now a pond with two hectares of crystal clear water, in some places up to twenty meters deep, teeming with fish, water snails, and freshwater crabs. All around it nature is coming back and we manage to grow our crops and have cattle, pigs, chicken, ducks, and guinea-fowl, while keeping one third of the land in recovering wilderness. Biological diversity is growing at a rate we never thought possible. Only when we show our visitors photographs of what this place was do they realize the incredible powers of regeneration of nature.

But this is not a happy ending, only a small seedling in the clearcut. The problem with poisons in agriculture may be a little less serious but it is still there, and it is getting more complicated. Now, allied with biotechnology, it threatens to initiate a replay of the Green Revolution. Few people, even in the ecology movement, seem to see what is happening. During a recent international meeting on biotechnology and farmers' rights, some of the participants put most

21

emphasis on "safeguards," thus implicitly accepting biotechnology as it is being introduced to agriculture by the same powers that forced the poisons.

This brings us to one of the most fundamental aspects of environmentalism today. If you want to be efficient, you must be knowledgeable. Otherwise there is danger of attacking at the wrong point or arguing on the wrong level – the level the powerful choose and on which they almost always win.

Years ago in our wine-growing region in the northeast of our state a very potent total herbicide was introduced. It had serious toxic effects on people and was therefore soon abandoned after having been in general use. The manufacturers reacted by insisting it was only a question of improper use, that farmers were not using protective clothing and masks, were not using the right concentrations at the right time, and so on. As so often, it is the victim who was blamed. Most farmers and agronomists were inclined to accept these arguments. I then argued as follows: even if this product were as harmless as distilled water, as good for health as mother's milk is for the baby, it still should never be used in our vineyards. I reminded the farmers, all descendants of Italian immigrants who came here in the middle of the last century, that their grandfathers, when they introduced wine growing here, did something quite different from what they did in Italy. There, in a much drier climate, they grew the vines on trellises, but here, on the rocky slopes where they lived and in our very humid climate, where weeds grow luxuriously when not controlled, they preferred a continuous arbor, high enough for cows or sheep to graze underneath. They kept a good green cover of rye grass with vetches and clovers. Their vines were healthy and the farmers used only the traditional, harmless copper-fungicides. The new herbicide, regardless of whether it presented toxicological problems, was a disaster because it destroyed the green cover that kept the vines healthy. The cattle had kept the grass short. So, instead of spending money on plant-killers, the farmer had free pasture. Most wine growers now keep their vineyards green again. But the herbicides also caused serious erosion, and with weakened vines, the farmers resorted to the new carbamate fungicides that cause still more problems, including more insidious toxicological ones.

In the case of biotechnology in agriculture today we also have a situation where many good people are fighting against the lesser part of the evil without seeing the great overall dangers. The Green Revolution caused the uprooting of millions of peasants worldwide and there was another, even more irreversible disaster: uncounted thousands of varieties of traditional cultivars were lost forever. In the case of rice, for instance, these varieties were the result of thousands of years of conscious or unconscious selection by the peasants themselves. Today we sow the same varieties in Louisiana, Hawaii, in southern Brazil and Uruguay, and in all of Southeast Asia. The same has happened to wheat, barley, rye, or maize; apples, pears, etc. In the Andean countries, Central America, and Mexico, Indian peasants cultivated an incredible wealth of varieties of potatoes. What survived the Green Revolution will soon be wiped out by biotechnology, when the same corporations that put the farmer in the position of total dependency on agri-chemicals succeed in making him equally dependent on their patented seeds, some of them selected not for resistance to pests, but resistance to pesticides. So it is nonsense to fight the planting out in the field of genetically engineered strawberries. They could never survive, much less spread out without our help. Most of our cultivars are plants that live, so to speak, in symbiosis with us humans. A field of maize or wheat not harvested cannot survive into the next year. Native vegetation will take over. Of course this does not apply to organisms that can survive in the wild, especially bacteria, fungi, and insects.

What we must now fight in biotechnology as now directed by big corporations is the patenting of living beings, parts of living beings, or processes with living beings. During the last two decades the same corporations that forced agricultural poisons onto the farmers have bought almost all the seed companies. They insist on patenting. Among other tools for making the farmer still more dependent on them, they are spending millions of dollars on research to put on the market patented seed that is already covered with layers of fertilizer, fungicides, insecticides, and a total herbicide that kills every plant that happens to be near but for which that particular patented seed is immune!

Legislation to foster such schemes is already on the books in many countries. In Brazil, until now, we have been able to prevent it. In Canada, Pat Mooney was the pioneer in making the world conscious of what is happening. In our parliament tremendous pressure is now being applied to our legislators to approve this kind of legislation. This time, we may lose.

Otherwise, there is nothing wrong with molecular biology and genetic engineering, but it should not be used to create still more structures of dependency. It could really bring great benefit if it was directed at true advantages for humanity. Suppose, among other things, we learned to really understand how genes control structure and growth, not just the synthesis of proteins. We might then be able to have an amputated arm grow back. This is still possible in frogs and other lower vertebrates; it just may be possible for us.

Agri-poisons and biotechnology are only part of the problem. Modern agriculture is not only ecologically pernicious and socially disastrous, it is just not the solution for the problem of feeding the human masses. Even if it can temporarily, with absurd subsidies, produce surpluses that then require additional subsidies to destroy, in the not very long term it will lead to total calamity. No process that builds on nonrenewable raw materials and energy can last very long. But it also is not as efficient as it pretends to be.

When comparing modern agriculture with traditional peasant cultures, it is always said that, while in the past forty to sixty per cent of the population had to work the land to feed itself and the rest, now, in First World countries, less than two per cent are sufficient; one farmer can feed fifty people. If this were true, we really would have no alternative. But it is a fallacy, when not a deliberate lie. When looked at systemically, traditional peasant agriculture was an autarchic system of production and distribution of food, that is, it produced its own inputs. The peasant produced his own fertilizer, dung from his animals, and his energy too. He used draft animals that grazed on his pasture or were fed hay or silage that also came from his soil: solar energy captured by photosynthesis. He also delivered the food he produced practically into the hands of the consumer at the weekly local market.

But what is the modern farmer? Not much more than a tractor driver and applier of chemicals. The individual farmer is a very small cog in an enormous and complex techno-bureaucratic structure that includes oil fields, refineries, mines, steel mills, aluminum smelters, big dams that flood rainforests and wipe out Indian tribes or uproot rubber tappers to make the electricity for the aluminium smelters, tool and tractor makers, combine and truck manufacturers, a sizable portion of the chemical industry and the banking system, agricultural schools, extension services, agricultural experiment stations, plus an industry that did not even exist before, the food manipulating, denaturing, and contaminating industry – and a lot more, such as all the packaging, deep freezing, pre-cooking, and what not.

So, if we want to compare the traditional farmer with the modern-day farmer we must compare the systems. How was food produced and distributed then and today? Modern economic macro-accounting doesn't make this kind of calculation. The different industries are seen as different parts of the economy and in the gross national product, only money flow is compared. If we compared the complete systems, we would certainly find that today, also, at least forty per cent of all working hours are for production and distribution of food. We would have to include the working hours necessary to earn the tax money that goes into the subsidies. Overall, we haven't really gained very much in terms of man-hour efficiency. What we have is a different distribution of tasks and a tremendous increase in environmental costs.

Of course, it can be argued that it is much more comfortable to sit in front of a computer in the bank than to trudge in the fields. But then, it need not to be as hard anymore as it was in the past. Intelligent organic farming, with the right crop rotation, companion planting, green manure, and integration of crops with animal husbandry, makes totally unnecessary what I still saw in Germany in the 1950s – women on all fours in sugarbeet fields pulling weeds with their hands. With today's comforts, life on the farm can be a lot more interesting, more humanly significant, and healthier than the lives of most city workers.

In the 1940s, when I studied agronomy, all agricultural research and experimentation was still directed toward organic methods. It was not the farmers who asked for a change in course, it was industry that imposed it on them. The banks, the schools, and the government catered to the interests of industry, not to the interests of farmers, of consumers, and of ecological sustainability.

Among the high environmental costs of modern agriculture are energy and raw materials. Traditional agriculture worked with solar energy via photosynthesis in its crops. Today it is fossil fuels and even nuclear power that goes into food production. Worse, agriculture now consumes more energy than it gets from the sun. This can be compared to an oil well that uses more energy in the pump than can be recovered from the oil pumped up. This kind of oil well is harmful for the economy as a whole, but it can be profitable for the owner if he is subsidized. That is why modern agriculture needs massive subsidies.

To make some of the fertilizers, enormous amounts of electricity and fossil fuels are used to fix nitrogen from the air in highly pressurized containers and at very high temperatures (Haber-Bosch process), a process that legumes do at ambient temperature with minimal energy use and with the help of certain bacteria on their roots, at no extra cost for the farmer. To make phosphorous fertilizers, phosphate mines are depleted at a rate that will exhaust them even before the oil is gone. Whole islands have been demolished in the Pacific.

The absurdity of modern food production systems is even more evident in intensive cattle, pig, and chicken rearing. Here we are faced with massive destruction of food for the sake of "vertical integration." The chicken slaughterhouse also owns the feed factory and the hatchery for the chicks. These are not even races anymore, they are registered chicken brands. The "producer" must buy all his inputs from the company, at prices they control, and he must sell his produce to the same people, again at prices they dictate! He may think he is a self-employed entrepreneur, but in fact he is a laborer with no guaranteed salary and no social security. These schemes have little to do with efficiency in production but very much with power structures, with developing techno-bureaucratic structures for the creation of dependency.

In the past, our farm animals produced the fertilizer to keep soils fertile; today, they produce waste. In Europe alone, hundreds of millions of tons of slurry – liquid cattle or pig manure – are treated as dirt. Until recently, much of it was simply dumped in the ocean. Now, when it is put back where it belongs, on the soil, it is done in ways that degrade, not improve, the soil. This leads to heavy leaching of nitrates into the subsoil and hence into wells, springs, brooks, and rivers, creating manifold health problems.

Where traditional agriculture worked with closed cycles just as ecosystems do, its modern counterpart opens cycles that should be kept closed. The fertility of our soils ends up in immense and growing garbage dumps and in the sewers. Some modern sewage treatment plants are now, on the pretext that the sludge is contaminated with heavy metals, drying it with high energy input, then burning it and dumping the ashes. Nothing could be more absurd!

And the animals in the feedlots, chicken concentration camps, and pig dungeons are fed grain and even – the height of lunacy – dried milk. Instead of complementing food production for humans on our fields, they now compete with us. They need extra crops, such as the soybean fields in southern Brazil for which the remaining subtropical rainforests in the Uruguay valley were wiped out, or tropical rainforests that are cleared in Asia to make way for manioc to make tapioca for the fat cows in Europe that produce the seas of milk and mountains of butter.

Peasant agriculture was sustainable forever. Modern agriculture is suicidal.

In October 1993, in Bangalore, India, at the opening of a conference on "Farmers' Intellectual Rights," there was a demonstration by half a million farmers against GATT, the World Bank, and biotechnology, and for sustainable farming. This gives us hope again. The leader of the Indian farmers said that, if necessary, he could bring twenty million people to New Delhi. The media almost totally ignored the event.

Why did the farmers protest against the World Bank and GATT? Because they realize these technocratic instruments threaten them by replacing small farmers with agribusiness everywhere. Even if they don't openly say so, that will be the result of the globalization of the economy. The uprising in Chiapas, Mexico, is for the same reason. NAFTA will make the survival of the Mexican peasant impossible. The Indian peasants will not be able to compete with American agribusiness. When American industrial workers protested as well, it was because they know that to the extent that real wages continue to go down in Mexico, with increasing migration to the cities, American big business will export jobs to Mexico, and American real wages will also continue to drop.

It is bad enough when European farmers are uprooted, as can now be observed in Spain or France. Old peasant wisdom is lost forever. In the Third World it is much worse. The Mexican peasants are Indians, descendants of the Mayas and Aztecs, with many different languages and cultures. When the village empties and the peasants languish in the slums of the cities, all is irreversibly lost; it is cultural genocide. This is what the Asian farmers in Bangalore knew could happen to them.

The globalization of the economy with GATT and the common markets is now threatening not just peasants and small farmers. The export of jobs to where labor costs are lowest is causing unemployment in the First World too. And worse than the destruction of jobs is the systematic disruption of all historically and systemically grown, stable, locally adapted, and sustainable social structures. Everywhere people are being massified and alienated, becoming uprooted, losing their traditional values and ideals, and being confronted with only the hedonistic, orgiastic ethics of modern advertising. Small wonder that even in wealthy countries such as Switzerland, children of rich families slide into the squalor of places such as Letten Station in

Zurich, where thousands of young people languish in filth and stupor, physically and mentally destroyed by hard drugs.

When conventional wisdom divides the world into rich and poor countries, what is usually left out out of the argument is the fact that the poor people of today were formerly not poor at all. While their traditional cultures were intact, with very few exceptions they were rich, rich in human fulfillment. What made them poor was development. Colonialism disrupted their solid social structures and demolished their economies, as when peasant farming for self-sufficiency was forced to give way to big plantation farming for export to the central powers.

This process continues today but the dominating powers are not governments any more and they do not have to send armies to occupy other peoples' land to install administrations of their own. Neocolonialism is much smarter and much, much more efficient. When I was Minister of the Environment in Brazil, I often had to face arguments by some of our military that the First World would eventually occupy Amazonia and take it away from us, that they wanted to have control of the minerals and other resources. "Nonsense," I replied. "It is you who are giving it to them on a silver platter. They would not be so foolish as to occupy it."

Years ago, in Africa, a man in Senegal said, "During colonial times the situation was transparent. When somebody spoke French and was white, I knew he was one of my exploiters. Now my worst enemies have my color of skin and speak my dialect."

A good example of neocolonialism is the Tucurì-Carajás complex. The First World, with its multilateral development banks, conceived, proposed and financed a huge dam that flooded three thousand square kilometers of pristine forest, finished off two Indian tribes, uprooted more than ten thousand rubber tappers and other forest dwellers, caused a series of other environmental disasters, some indirectly triggered by it, such as the destruction of more than a hundred thousand square kilometers of virgin forest (an area larger than Portugal or Austria) and cost the Brazilian people an additional indebtedness of over six billion dollars. What was this dam for? The electricity, only some eight hundred megawatts, goes to multinational aluminum smelters and is delivered to them below production costs. Why? Because the smelters can argue that they need subsidized electricity to compete with low world-market prices for aluminum. But why is the price of aluminum so low? Because of the surplus production of the Tucurì-Carajás scheme! So what do we have? The First

World imposes and finances a scheme that makes it possible for it to get resources from the Third World at ridiculously low prices and the Third World pays all the costs – social, environmental and financial. No occupation of foreign land is necessary.

In neocolonialism the central powers are diffuse and the situation is much more complicated. It is not the British, French, or Dutch, or even the Germans and Italians anymore, it is the transnational corporations and they do not really belong anywhere. Today they are the centers of technology development and the technologies they develop and impose are not necessarily conceived to satisfy true human needs, they are conceived in their interest, to conquer markets and to solidify and amplify their power.

So we need a political and ecological critique of technology. Even among environmentalists, many do not realize what is happening. Politicians are either ignorant or collusive. When we fought poisons in agriculture, we were addressing misguided technologies. The requirement of prescription for the sale of pesticides is a technical fix; so is registration and other controlling legislation. We must now go much deeper. Of course technical fixes are important and necessary. For some industries that is all we need, but technical fixes are not always sufficient. We must rethink all our technology, not only in agriculture, but also in energy generation, in transportation, industry, health, and sanitation, and especially in education.

In the case of agriculture, the long term solution is organic agriculture, or, to use a more appropriate term, regenerative agriculture. Fortunately, it has already progressed to the point where it cannot be marginalized any more by those powerful corporations and institutions that feel threatened by it. Now, even they are reluctantly paying lip-service to it. Here, renewed and massive activity, a lot of practical work, is now necessary. Millions of young people who yearn for morally significant activity, and many older people too, can participate with enthusiasm. Consumers everywhere are also becoming more aware and are asking for clean, health-promoting food.

This effort could be helped and accelerated by a new orientation in sanitary engineering. Today it concentrates mostly on megatechnological and centralizing solutions, such as incineration or gigantic dumps where garbage and rubble are compacted and isolated and the area "recultivated," all at very high cost, up to hundreds of dollars per ton. In the case of toxic stuff the cost can go up to thousands of dollars per ton, when it is not openly or covertly exported to Third World countries (or even dumped in the ocean). In the case of radioactive materials the situation is such that nobody has found a final disposal solution yet.

The new orientation would not start from the premise that we want to get rid of what we call dirt, garbage, waste, etc., but that we want, first, to produce as little waste as possible and then to recycle whatever can be reused – that is, we want to work with closed cycles, the way living systems always do. This applies first of all to the hundreds of millions of tons of precious organic matter that are discarded annually from slaughterhouses; from canning factories for meat, fruit, vegetables, and fish; from wine cellars, breweries, tanneries, and sawmills – all that goes into urban garbage dumps and sewers, as well as all the slurry from intensive cattle, pig, and chicken operations. While this monumental waste continues, while most of the stuff is handled in ways that either contaminate it or make recycling impossible, hundreds of millions of hectares of good soil are degraded every year with unnecessary mechanical tilling, causing erosion, and with massive use of chemical fertilizers and downpours of poisons – all practices that destroy soil life and drastically lower the humus content. The soils are starving for organic matter while industry and cities are destroying it. This situation must be reversed. The cycles we have opened must be closed again. This is another great field of activity for millions of intelligent people, an activity from which uncounted numbers of NGOs and even businesses could prosper.

Modern medicine has become a multibillion dollar industry that operates on the same principle that keeps the repair shops for cars going: let the cars break down and we will repair them, preferably by exchanging spare parts. It has now become so technologically sophisticated and so expensive that most health care systems are breaking down. Here too we need a new orientation, where prevention counts more than repair. Prevention means healthy food and healthy life styles. Agriculture, industry, and health care must be linked in a way quite opposite to how they are linked today, where industry contributes to a sick form of agriculture which, therefore, produces food that makes us sick.

But our present environmental predicament is not just a problem of technology gone astray. The problem is there because the technologies are efficient, as efficient as their owners want them to be. It is not a question of too many bandaids, either. Most serious damage is done by well-meaning people. Better filters on our chimneys and exhausts, more efficient sewage treatment stations, healthier and more sustainable agriculture, cleaner food processing, more recycling of wastes, more and bigger nature reserves: all this will help, but it is not enough. It will not save our descendants.

We must reexamine our aims. What is progress, what is development? What is technology for? How are we going to put civilization back in step with creation and at the same time make a just society?

I remember reading, decades ago, an essay by Bertrand Russell. It was a thought experiment that, in essence, went like this: Suppose in an economy there is a certain number of pin factories. They produce all the pins the people need. Everybody is satisfied, both those who need the pins and those who manufacture them. Then, somebody invents a machine that makes it possible to produce the same number of pins in half the time, other factors remaining equal. What would be the intelligent, socially desirable thing to do? All the pin factories should use this machine and work only half time with the same income, the same wages and salaries. Workers and executives would have more time for leisure, for fun, for cultivating friendships and love, for sports, arts, music, the enjoyment of nature, and so on. Other industries would find and apply similar innovations. Technological progress would thus contribute to gradual improvement in comfort for everybody, society would become more humane, there would be more culture and beauty, and nature would be more protected, as we would use fewer and fewer resources. But what happens in practice? They all buy the new machines and everybody tries to produce and sell twice as much as before. Fierce competition ensues, half the factories go bankrupt, half the jobs are lost. In the end, the same number of pins are used but there is more despair, frustration, and unhappiness.

Of course, this is an oversimplified metaphor, but it illustrates how technology that could contribute to more freedom and contentment, as well as less environmental impact, more often than not has the opposite effect.

My father, who lived from the 1880s to the 1950s, could hardly have imagined all the time-saving devices we have today, but he certainly could not have understood how short of time we are today despite all the computers, faxes, modems, printers, photocopiers, global satellite transmission, high speed trains and planes, expressways, and what not. The only time-saving contraption he had was a phone and he boarded a plane only once in his lifetime. But he led a beautifully productive life. As an architect and building contractor he left behind artistic buildings and churches. He was also a professor at an art school, and produced many precious paintings that portrayed the life of the Gaucho, the cowboy of the Pampa, of the colonists in our peasant regions, and also life in the cities. All of them are of historical value now, in a style somewhat like Norman Rockwell, except that he painted only for fun. He never sold his paintings, he kept them or gave them away. And what profound satisfaction he got out of it all!

Ecological awareness must now go beyond confrontation and technical fixes, beyond even fundamental reformulation of technology and technological infrastructures.

Most important and certainly most difficult of all is the necessary rethinking of our cosmology. The anthropocentric world view Westerners inherited from our remote Judeo-Christian past has allowed our technocrats and bureaucrats, and most simple people, too, to look at Planet Earth as if it were no more than a free storehouse of unlimited resources to be used, consumed and wasted for even our most absurd or stupid whims. We have no respect for creation. Nothing in nature is sacred. Nothing, except us humans, has sufficient inherent value not to have to yield when "economic" or other human interests dictate it. Mountains can be razed, rivers turned around, forests flooded or annihilated, unique life forms or whole living systems eliminated without qualms, or patented for personal or institutional power.

How else could it be that even with a man like Al Gore in the Vice-Presidency of the United States and with all the worldwide concern about the wholesale devastation of tropical rainforests, the final demolition of the Pacific temperate rainforest cannot be halted? Economists see creation of wealth only in the money earned in the export from the rape of the forest, while deducting nothing in their accounts of national wealth for the total and irreplaceable loss of the whole ecosystem. For them only the abstraction we call money is real and they think they can even create it out of nothing to produce the necessary technologies that, miraculously, will help us overcome all imaginable shortages and devastations. Funny, those who least understand science and technology are the ones who most expect from it, to the point of believing we can go on acting in the most irresponsible ways forever.

A beautiful coincidence: While writing this, early in the morning of September 19, 1994 – spring in the Southern Hemisphere – at a table in front of my cottage on Gaia-Corner, I feel a fleeting shadow passing me on the ground, then another. Looking up, I see a pair of storks. They came straight from the rising sun. After soaring in three large circles over our pond they continue their flight due west. This is reality! How not to feel profound reverence?

How are we going to spread the new – actually very, very old – holistic ethics the planet now needs for the marvellous process of organic evolution to be allowed to unfold unhampered again?

The human brain has the capacity to become an agent for increasing creativity within the flow of life or it can continue disrupting it until it is too late, until points of no return have been overshot.

With very few exceptions indigenous peoples (those we like to call "primitive") developed mythologies, taboos, rituals, and attitudes that made their existence compatible with the survival of the ecosystems they depended on, sometimes even enriching them. In modern terminology we would say their life styles were sustainable. Modern global industrial civilization, though, is fundamentally unsustainable. It has now imposed on what remains of traditional cultures the ethics of the gold miner who takes what he can from a place where he has no roots, who refrains from no devastation in order to get to his bonanza and, when there is nothing left of interest to him, leaves without remorse.

We need a new frame of reference, to put it in more technical terms. If I said "mythology" many scientifically-minded people might protest. James Lovelock suffered stinging attacks from people who thought he was too emotional. But his concept of Gaia, the Earth as a homeostatic system that regulates itself so that environmental factors such as temperature range, salinity, redox-effect, acidity, mixture of gases in the atmosphere, cloudiness, etc., remain within what is appropriate for life, lends itself both to a strictly scientific interpretation and to more mythological ways of looking at the world, which is what most people need.

The most urgent and noble task of NGOs now is to mobilize all the forces that can contribute to the necessary change in world view. Our modern technologies of communication and publicity make it possible. The political will to do it can only come from below, from the citizen.

Part One:
Education

3

Educating the Executive and Students

Kris McDivitt

There are no textbooks available on how to operate a business in an ecologically sustainable way. However, there are a handful of companies today that are ecological pioneers while at the same time being very successful in business terms. One of these ecological pioneer companies is Patagonia, the premier maker of outdoor clothing and equipment.

From its beginnings in the early seventies to its present size with gross sales exceeding $100 million, Patagonia has been committed to producing equipment of the highest quality, valuing its employees for their uniqueness and diversity, and demonstrating a strong concern for the environment. Its five-year environmental goals include environmental accounting, eliminating all solid waste from domestic facilities, increasing awareness of product impact, working with suppliers to meet environmental standards, and reducing the use of paper and energy while expanding that of sustainable paper products and forms of energy. In addition, the company has embraced environmental activism, donating 1% of its sales to environmental causes.

Kris McDivitt served as CEO of Patagonia for fifteen years, during which she helped guide the organization on the path toward sustainability. In this chapter McDivitt remembers how she gradually became aware that traditional executive attitudes and decision-making methods, including some of her own, were fatally out of step with contemporary reality – particularly with environmental reality. She recounts her unsatisfying experiences in trying to get up to speed through education in a leading business school, and draws challenging conclusions as to how business education must be reshaped if it is to serve executives, society, and a sustainable world.

McDivitt's reflections are a passionate testimony of an executive who wishes to do more than just do good business. She offers this testimony so that many other executives who find themselves in similar situations will not have to reinvent the wheel she designed and put into practice over all those years.

McDivitt to CEO: "What do you think of when you hear the term sustainability?"

CEO: "Keeping our profits above 11%, year in, year out."

McDivitt: "Ah ... I see."

All social and educational reforms must be assessed in terms of whether they mitigate or exacerbate the ecological crisis.

—C.A. Bowers

In order for there to be a substantive shift in direction within the corporate community, tending away from the current world market system oriented towards never ending growth and profits and moving toward a more sustainable future, executives must agree that there is an environmental and social crisis in the first place. Today, among the world's corporate executives, we do not have consensus on this. We have instead what Fritjof Capra describes as a "crisis of perception" within the ranks of business leaders and among the thousands of students in business schools throughout the world. These people will be expected to take part in the ever-expanding role of business as it increasingly determines the fates of governments, communities, and even families. The degree to which our nation's political leaders, corporate leaders, and top economists fail to understand this crisis, or choose to ignore it, is truly alarming given current signs of near total ecological collapse of our natural resources and distress signals of mammoth proportions that our cities are disintegrating. Indeed, we are in the throes of a potentially fatal crisis of perception, and business, particularly transnationals, is exacerbating the social and ecological crisis we find ourselves in today.

One of the ways in which we can begin to bridge the gap between reality and perception is through better education of the people who are often blinded or misinformed by their distance from ecological and social reality – corporate executives. As a corporate executive myself, I have sought out such education.

Unfortunately, the governmental and private institutions funding our universities and promoting private think tanks on global business do not realize that we are on the brink of real ecological and social collapse – or, if they are prepared to admit that we are failing in some way, they are sure that all our problems can be "fixed" by new and better technologies. Generally speaking, there is no conscious awareness within our culture that we live on this planet as a guest, not as the host. We have long been inculculated with the concept that the earth, her natural resources, and the other species co-existing with us exist solely to support humans and our development. So long as we believe this, and have an unquestioned trust and belief in technology to support us, we create an almost unthinkably difficult situation for the re-education of business executives and students within today's educational arena.

Formal education for business executives should begin in kindergarten. Barring that, the re-education of CEOs doing business within our consumer culture can and must begin by careful examination of the effects of businesses on cultures, the natural world, and the species living within it.

My own re-education began to take form after sharing the leadership of our successful business for 15 years, watching with a kind of fascination as its growth tilted upward each year and our profits glided upwards with it. Not being among the MBA-possessing elite, I began to suspect that I was unprepared to be running as large a company as I found myself running. I was unwilling to trust experience over schooling, so I signed up for a program at Stanford University for "executive training." Stanford University's business school is considered one of the leading institutions of its type, and I had high hopes that it would teach me what I needed to know. I was utterly unprepared for my discovery that business school is no place to learn about business; in fact, school was part of what I was beginning to recognize as the problem with business. At the end of my term at Stanford I wrote a long, frustrated letter to the head of the program, outlining my dismay. Among other things, I wrote, at extraordinary cost of time and money I was handed old, out-of-date ideas served up by tired tenured professors who were at best theorists, never having been out working in corporations day to day; instead, they sat there on the campus supporting the dominant view in order to protect their jobs. The experience gave me, I wrote, a new understanding that our university system exists in large part to support and provide continuity to a world view that represents the consumer culture. Until this point (naively) I had seen the upper level of formal education as being relatively independent of social, economic, and philosophical bias – rather as I had thought our small-town newspaper was independent until I was old enough to see that the voice of that paper was simply the voice of its owner. Perhaps most importantly, sitting through those classes I saw firsthand that in all their evaluating of profit and loss, tips on how to increase efficiency in production and distribution, ideas on marketing to new customers, and suggestions for "motivating the workforce," there was no discussion of business in the context of its profound effects on society worldwide and its impact on our natural world and the millions of species within it. Alternative resource-based accounting principles were never even mentioned, never mind discussed in depth. There was no debate, no review of the simple concept of limitation, a concept which one of Patagonia's chief shareholders had been clamoring about for years: the limits of our natural resources, limits to the number of "customers" the earth can support, limits to the sheer size of any business. The idea of corporate responsibility of any kind was not a topic. Nor was the idea that corporations have, over time, been given more "rights" than an individual, so that we as their leaders have a responsibility to behave in the best interests of our immediate work community, our regional community, and the natural world at large.

In my business school experience, and I am sure it was not unique, these urgent matters were not in the curriculum, and not even topics of informal conversation or debate. Yet these are just a few of the realities that desperately need to be addressed in front of executives and business school students at every point in their education.

Instead, students are systematically excluded from crucial knowledge: that we are in an ever-deepening ecological crisis unparalleled in history, that the number of species going extinct is an astounding 137 per day or roughly 50,000 species per year, that the social degeneration and rapid decline of family and community cohesiveness is nearing explosive dimensions, that the air we breathe, the water we drink, and the food we eat are often bad for our health and increasingly held in great mistrust by the public. *Progress*, as we have defined it over the past 60 years and *prosperity* as we have raced after it for as many years has not, in fact, raised the quality of our lives as a society. (Clearly, some of the world's population – perhaps .01% – through their vast accumulation of wealth are enjoying life just fine; however, they do so by having enough money to avoid the realities of their communities.) If we can agree that these points are generally true, then clearly we can agree that a general alarm must be sounded within our educational system – that there must be a long and deep discussion at every level, resounding debate, and the clamor of concern and evaluation between teachers and students. There is not. Within the departments of sociology, ecology, and biology, you will find plenty of wise voices acknowledging these crises and how they are linked together. However, it has been my experience that you will find no mention of these ideas within the MBA programs in our business school.

Why is there no debate regarding our natural resources being used up at breakneck speed, resources upon which most of our businesses are either directly or indirectly relying? Why no discussion of our unsustainable habits, which no number of technological breakthroughs will change? Business executives attending workshops, seminars, classes, even private tutorials are not hearing from their lecturers that the organizations they oversee are based on an economic model of unlimited growth and multinational proliferation that cannot, will not, be sustained over the long run.

What are the real prospects that face us? As David Ehrenfeld writes so perceptively in *Beginning Again*, "A more likely cause of upheaval is the disintegration of the extremely complicated and finicky economic, industrial, social, and political structure that we have put together in the decades since the Second World War. This structure has been supported by resources, especially petroleum, that are waning, and by an environmental and cultural legacy – soil, vegetation, air, water, families, traditions – that we so foolishly took for granted, squandered and lost.

"The visible agent of this change would be a global economic collapse. Such a collapse would probably disrupt international trade, trigger the disintegration of many multinational corporations and other overstuffed, subsidized super-organizations, end the modern welfare state, diminish governmental regulatory supervision (including environmental regulations), bring about massive famines and movements of populations, greatly increase unemployment in the industrialized nations, all but eliminate luxury goods and exceedingly complex manufacturers, including many advanced military weapons, hasten the spread of new and old epidemic diseases, trigger the inevitable population crash, and cause a proliferation of regional economic, social and political systems." I have been a guest at some of the top university business schools in the United States and not once have I heard it mentioned that we live in a society gone out of control.

In the hundreds (if not thousands) of seminars and classrooms filled to talk about "management" – managing your people in ten minutes, managing time, managing more effectively, men managing women, women managing men, managing money, managing "down" – you will find no discussion of what Ehrenfeld calls "the over-managed society." There is an extraordinary proliferation of managers in our society, says Ehrenfeld, an ever-increasing percentage of people who control other people but do not themselves produce anything real or useful. The problem of the growth of management and its influence can be seen in nearly every area of modern life. Yet you will not hear of this in the schools.

Students and executives are still being drilled on the virtues of the path toward growth and ever-higher profits, learning strategies for global expansion and how to use an ever-expanding computerized communications link-up around the world. There are few, if any, schools bringing to the forefront the raw facts that the profit and growth curves we seek are not limitless and that global expansion of transnationals is in fact creating environmental and social disintegration. Within the massive and almost unavoidable infrastructure surrounding computers and computerization, we find no thoughtful advice for us, no deep analysis of what the effects of our use of the computer within our businesses actually is.

In reality, the introduction of computers has brought about an extraordinary acceleration of our use of the earth's resources and has brought us to the edge of their depletion, but that is not part of today's curriculum. Executives need help in thinking about such things, but we do not get it from the educators. For example, at Patagonia we have installed e-mail, perhaps without seriously considering how this technological development might change the basic manner in which we communicate with each other – probably changing the basic culture we are so happy with in ways we will find destructive of human relationships, intimacy, trust, and creativity. We corporate leaders, like many others within our technological culture, are accepting out of hand that technological change means progress and progress necessarily means "better." Surely all of us need to be keenly aware of, if not in agreement with, the opposing viewpoint that technological advancements often have destructive effects on our companies as well as on the planet and its human and natural communities.

As robotization accelerates, we have not focused clearly on the darker side of creating ever greater "efficiencies" and "productivity" in our workforce: that it leads to a rapidly shrinking number of jobs, which will lead to communities, families, and individuals left jobless, marginalized – and unable to buy our products. We are cannibalizing the very consumers we depend upon for our sales of goods and services.

In looking at the educational process and curriculum of some schools we see that, in general, the current near-sightedness only reflects the general lack of attention paid outside our schools as well. It is my opinion as a business leader and as someone with some experience lecturing within the business school system about which I speak that, in fact, it will be extremely difficult to challenge the traditionally held viewpoint that is being taught in our educational system. As glaring examples, let me describe two situations outside the business schools:

(1) Chris Maser, author, lecturer, and international consultant on sustainable forestry with 20 years of experience, cites this example: "I was a guest lecturer in a forest management class in which I discussed large woody debris, small mammals, mycorrhizal fungi, nutrient cycling, and the effects of gross habitat alterations in coniferous forests. When the class was over, a young student came straight at me so angry his fists were clenched and his face was red. 'I'm a senior,' he shouted, 'and I'm going to graduate in a couple of weeks. How come this is the first time I've heard any of this? I've just spent four years in what they call forest management! You just showed me that I don't know a damn thing about how a forest works! And now I'm supposed to be a forester! What in the hell am I going to do out there!' This young man was astute enough when given opposing information to let his intuition speak and thereby penetrate dogma's armor and see the economic lie of forest management. But as far as his university training was concerned, the truth came late."

(2) Within the University of California system, in the heart of what is still the chief supplier of our nation's food, you will not find in the agriculture college a formal and legitimized division concentrating on the development of organic growing models; the only exception is the small and essentially self-financed agro-ecology school on the Santa Cruz campus. The situation within the business schools is essentially no different and thus we find ourselves confronting growing ecological, economic, and social disintegration with little help coming from the very institutions whose charter supposedly lies in readying their charges for the future we face.

Anyone can identify destructive forest practices. You don't have to be a professional forester to recognize bad forestry any more than you have to be a doctor to recognize ill health. If logging looks bad, it is bad. If a forest appears to be mismanaged, it is mismanaged.

> – Gordon Robinson, head forester,
> Southern Pacific Railroad, 1939–66

A badly managed company is as obvious as a badly managed forest. Are some corporate leaders and students sensing that all is not well in the kingdom? I think so. Over the past seven years I have observed a trend, albeit a very slow one, in interest from students in front of whom I've spoken. Perhaps only on an instinctual level, the underpinnings of corporate life are beginning to make less and less sense and hold up less and less well to scrutiny. Common sense makes students skeptical, I think, and when someone from the ranks of the business community essentially confirms to them what they suspect on their own, there is visible enthusiasm for more discussion. Moreover, in my recent experience in talking to students, some of them are understanding clearly that we bear responsibility to our communities and to the world at large.

We cannot reorient the entire educational system from kindergarten forward, but it is past time to begin to infuse strong, well-founded counter views into the classical business education. In its role of uncritically supporting the current economic system, business education in fact helps to keep it disfunctional. To believe that any business is capable of complete sustainability is, in my opinion, a delusion. However, between our current global market concepts and total sustainability lies tremendous room for aggressive and effective change in mindset and goals for corporate executives and students following in their footsteps.

The time has come to begin weaving into our business schools the kind of information and discussions that I so sorely missed and needed to have as the CEO of Patagonia. As proud as I am of what we have built as a company and as strong as Patagonia continues to be, I see its possibilities for being so much more as staggering. And, of course, the message that executives send through a company does not stop there; it filters out through your family, community, and even nation. We can set in motion positive benefits that reach as far into the planetary ecosystem as our negative impacts do.

I am not a professional educator and I do not pretend to understand the complete range of possibilities in educating students. However, on the strength of what I have realized that I need to know, and what I need executives to know who might work for me, I make the following recommendations for either supplementing or replacing teaching in business schools today:

(1) First and foremost, whether we are looking at an entire curriculum for a full-term business school or a simple three-day workshop for executives, topics must bridge several fields of study. Business is not an isolated realm but part of a much larger system within which it functions. Build sessions weaving biology, philosophy, history, ecology, anthropology, and economics together. It is essential that we figure out how to articulate our business interdependence with everything else. It is necessary to show that corporations are not islands unto themselves – the decisions I make sitting at my desk trigger an almost incalculable number of reactions.

(2) Each student of business should learn not only how to account for profit and loss but be given at least two or three courses on accounting for our natural resources. Our forests, soils, oceans, rivers, air, mountains, and lakes are, in the end, as critical to the long-term survival of our company as our inventory levels, employees, and growth curve and yet we do not see the connection.

(3) Having understood what resources are and what there is out there, we CEOs need to know how many of them have been used up, not to be replenished. What resources are being used at rates exceeding their carrying capacity? The devastation of our tropical and temperate rainforests, the extinction of species, the rapid rate at which our nation's prime top soil is being eroded, all these "resource assessments" need to be brought onto the desks of every chief executive whose company operations affect them – and almost all of our operations do. We should each be schooled on the cause-and-effect relationships between our corporations and the undoing of our ecosystems. Shifting the consumer culture away from its traditional ways is, admittedly, wrenching and difficult. But change is within our grasp more often than we imagine. For example, had we at Patagonia understood twenty years ago that conventional cotton was one of the most toxics-intensive, water-consuming materials, would we have used it to the extent that we do? Would we have avoided the predicament we are now in, of racing around trying to find alternatives to industrial cotton? Generally speaking, business leaders are not the Darth Vaders we are made out to be, but rather, as a group, enormously uninformed. I have faith that, given all of the information (though perhaps a repeated dose is necessary) we corporate leaders will begin, even if sometimes grudgingly, to shift our decision-making toward committing fewer non-sustainable acts.

(4) An enormously urgent point that urgently needs making in every lecture hall in every business school is that of the extermination of indigenous cultures around the world as they are rapidly absorbed into the global consumer culture. My own personal understanding of this disaster has changed my business strategic direction almost 180 degrees. In the 1970s, when Coca-Cola began its global campaign on television, every night I watched the magical blending of nationalities singing "I'd like to teach the world to sing in perfect harmony ..." and I was right there, somehow associating that vision with world peace and love. Today I don't see it that way. In 1984, while trekking near the upper borders of Nepal, I noticed a Nepalese man trundling along barefooted carrying a tall stack of twigs on his back – and sporting a Patagonia jacket over his traditional Nepali robe. At the time, how proud I was that even in the farthest corners of the world I could find someone wearing one of our products – even though it was almost certainly the gift of some earlier tourist! Now, however, I see that the most frightening results of our "success" in marketing our products lie in the monoculturalization of the world. We must acknowledge this counterproductive result of transnational business, within business schools and in our business lives. Using myself as an example, I would not necessarily make the same marketing decisions today that I did some fifteen years ago. We must always seek to understand the true ramifications of our actions.

(5) I am not a supporter of the case-study method; however, I do not think it will go away. So I suggest including the following kinds of case studies in the future:

- Take a single large industrial fisheries business and study the long-term effects their methods of fishing have on their business. Do the same study on the independent, small-scale fisherman and compare the effects of the two types of fishing.
- Develop a case study on the long-term activities of one of North America's largest lumber companies and push their business model out into the future.
- Take also the case study of the Northern Atlantic and Pacific salmon; develop the same framework for one of the dying indicator species on our planet. Forget about the study of the North Chicago Bank, dated around 1961; it is no of use to us. Relevance is in the interconnected planetary reality we find ourselves in today. We should be using case studies that exemplify the real nature of our businesses and the world we are doing business in.

(6) Business leaders (and students too) should understand first-

hand the interdependence between corporations and ecosystems. A surprising number of CEOs have never visited the sites where their products are produced (or discarded). Field trips to the dark side of production and disposal would begin to give us a more complete picture, supplementing the glamorous side of business. One rarely forgets the floating dead fish in the standing water or the parched and dead lands of a clearcut forest.

(7) Make the study of contemporary critiques of technology a mandatory part of our business education. Real education requires that we hear from the growing number of serious thinkers and social activists who are developing a sound analysis of the effects of megatechnologies; we CEOs and students must come to terms with this burgeoning critique.

(8) The study of the philosophy and history of our current western world view is an important groundwork from which a better understanding of how we got into this ecological mess in the first place will come. It is perhaps clearer in business than in any other area of human activity that apparently abstract ideas have real-world consequences.

(9) The work being done by economists in developing new ways of analyzing our nation's GNP should be woven into economics courses all along the way, beginning with lower division courses. A new generation of economists (among them Herman Daly) has begun to develop a new economic doctrine that can deal with the resource flows of the real world.

(10) Open up the doors and windows of the classrooms. Let the winds of the growing number of thinkers and activists from around the world speak to these centers of education. Allow the dominant world view to be scrutinized, poked at, and let the counter points that I so lacked in my years as CEO of Patagonia through the door. For instance, every CEO and business student should have to sit through the four-minute video *The Faceless Ones* (Western Canada Wilderness Committee, 20 Water Street, Vancouver BC V6B 1A4; fax 604-683-8229), which presents powerfully and succinctly the essence of the problem we face in creating more sustainability in business.

We always have to start somewhere, and starting small is still starting. At Patagonia we have always considered making hundreds of small improvements the right approach, rather than trying to take a few giant strides. I consider this to be one of the reasons we are on our way to a smaller number of non-sustainable acts.

Kris McDivitt's Reading List

The Arrogance of Humanism, David Ehrenfeld (Oxford University Press, 1975)
Beginning Again, David Ehrenfeld (Oxford University Press, 1993)
Four Arguments for the Elimination of Television, Jerry Mander (Quill, 1978)
In the Absence of the Sacred, Jerry Mander (Sierra Club, 1991)
Monocultures of the Mind, Vandana Shiva (Zed, 1993)
Ancient Futures, Helena Norberg-Hodge (Sierra Club, 1991)
Deep Ecology for the 21st Century, George Sessions, Ed. (Shambhala, 1995)
Where the Wasteland Ends, Theodore Roszak (Celestial Arts, 1989)
Education, Cultural Myths, and the Ecological Crisis, C.A. Bowers (SUNY, 1993)
Regarding Nature, Andrew McLaughlin (SUNY Press, 1993)
For the Common Good, Herman Daly and John Cobb (Beacon, 1994)
A Sand County Almanac, Aldo Leopold (Oxford UP, 1981)
The Debt Boomerang, Susan George (Inst. of Policy Studies, 1992)
Lords of Poverty, Graham Hancock (Grove-Atlantic, 1992)
The Development Dictionary, Wolfgang Sachs, Ed. (Zed, 1992)
Deschooling Society, Ivan Illich (Harper & Row, 1971)
Entropy, Jeremy Rifkin (Viking, 1980)
The End of Work, Jeremy Rifkin (Tarcher, 1995)
Global Ecology, Wolfgang Sachs (ZED, 1993)
"Four Changes," Gary Snyder (in *Turtle Island,* New Directions, 1974)
Limits to Growth, Donella Meadows et al. (Universe, 1972)
The End of Nature, Bill McKibben (Random House, 1989)
Technological Society, Jacques Ellul (Random House, 1967)
The Cult of Information, Theodore Roszak (University of California Press, 1994)
Technopoly, Neil Postman (Knopf, 1992)

4

The Learning Process Within Corporations

Oscar Motomura

Businesses are increasingly realizing that the challenges of moving toward sustainability require a major reorientation of management skills and attitudes. Oscar Motomura is the founder and CEO of the Amana-Key Group in Brazil, which assists both large and small companies and their executives in this process. Originally a consulting group in the area of business strategy, Amana-Key now specializes in business education, generating "knowledge products" for Brazilian executives. After its change of focus in the early eighties, Amana-Key expanded its customer base considerably, and today most of Brazil's largest corporations do business with the group through one or more of its product lines.

Recognizing that the transition to sustainability is arduous, Motomura offers in this chapter a flexible repertoire of techniques that companies and individual executives can benefit from in acquiring the new information, planning techniques, and learning/coaching strategies they need. The chapter concludes with an outline of Amana-Key's Systemic Executive Development Program, which explicitly incorporates the eight ecological principles presented by Fritjof Capra in our introductory chapter.

Increasingly companies have begun to use the kind of techniques suggested by Motomura to embark on radical environmental programs. For example, Södra Cell, a cooperative owned by 30,000 forest land owners in southern Sweden, has decided to produce totally chlorine-free paper. They based their decision on consumer demand, not on scientific proofs. Since the most demanding customers wished to have paper that did not contribute at all to the production and dis-

charge of dioxin, the company fulfilled that wish regardless of the scientific debates.

As soon as the totally chlorine-free paper was introduced, there was a massive demand for it, especially from Germany where almost all customers wanted to switch to the new paper. While American paper companies, such as Georgia Pacific, questioned the justification for chlorine-free paper with scientific arguments, the market swiftly turned toward the new product. Now Södra Cell has set the bench mark case in pulp production, and its competitors have no other option than to follow suit. In fact, the Swedish paper companies today enjoy a competitive edge not only in the sales of their pulp but also in the exports of the corresponding machinery.

Another illustrative case is Canon, the Japanese maker of cameras and photocopiers, which has engraved the principle of sustainability into its research and development policies. Since batteries are always an environmental hazard, Canon is now testing flexible amorphous solar cells to be placed in camera shoulder straps, which could provide energy without affecting the environment.

As metals are difficult to recycle when combined with plastics, all metals have been eliminated from Canon cameras; copiers are being redesigned in such a way that most of their parts can be reused; and all lead has been eliminated because of its well-known toxicity. Canon claims that these steps are only the beginning. This type of leadership is certainly unique and is bound to result in a significant competitive advantage for Canon.

If more and more companies are beginning to embrace the concept of ecological sustainability and to embark on radical environmental programs, this is in no small measure due to educators like Oscar Motomura, who is considered one of Brazil's most innovative strategic thinkers in management. Being able to rely on a wide range of expertise and skills, Motomura combines ecological awareness and a shrewd business sense with a unique ability to put all antagonism aside, and thus is able to guide business toward sustainability at the boardroom level in eminently practical ways.

Introduction

A textile company changes its industrial processes: it replaces non-ecological chemical supplies with "clean" alternatives and starts to use biophotodegradable materials in the packaging of its products.

A furniture company decides to use only plantation pine wood in its products in order to help reduce the destruction of rainforests.

A retail organization decides to stop offering its customers products that cannot be considered fully ecologically sound.

From the business standpoint, is it "strategic" to be ecologically correct in these times of changing values? Or is it a burden that can make business endeavors not feasible from an economic point of view (or at least make things harder than they already are)?

Business executives, consultants, academics, specialists, and politicians can spend much time debating that issue – trying to arrive at a "conclusion," a right answer. Nevertheless, from the bottom-line standpoint, that is not an "academic" question. It looks like a typical business decision, involving risk and rewards.

If that assumption is accepted, business concerns have three possible courses of action regarding ecology and sustainability. The first one is to become an ecologically oriented company. It is to "bet" on ecology as an inevitable trend. The rewards will be represented by finer attuning to the new customers' values, thus harvesting better results in the marketplace.

A second course of action is not to become an ecologically oriented company. Or in an even more aggressive bet, to plot strategies to "take advantage" of competitors that are trying to become ecologically sound. The risk here is to be caught in the future by irate consumers and regulators, and to face significant problems in sales, public image, and bottom-line results. The rewards may be represented by higher profits, at least in the short term, if ecology turns out to be just another fad.

A third alternative is to muddle through, to "wait and see." The risk factors here are not entirely different from those for companies of the second group above. Today time is a strategic resource. Ecologically-driven investments have long cycles in many industries and the choice to be a "follower" entails higher risks than presumed by superficial analysis. The rewards of this policy can only be short-term savings and an insignificant effect on long-term results; no actual bet is made in such an approach.

We can, however, approach the issue of ecology from a different standpoint. Our view is that we ought to lead that discussion to a higher level of consciousness, beyond the "bottom line/market share" perspective.

Ecology and sustainability are fundamental issues for life, rather than mere business factors. It is like the discussion of ethics in business. We still have businesspeople arguing that corporations cannot survive if they are to do business ethically or if they fully respect the rights of the consumers or if they are to care for the quality of life of their employees or if they are to contribute to solving community problems.

We all should learn about ecology and sustainability the same way that we should have been educated in ethics and values. In fact, we should go way beyond "literacy." It is our thinking that once businesspeople become fully aware of what deep ecology is all about, the "adjustments" in corporations will be a natural consequence, rather than a "business decision" based on pros and cons.

This chapter, based on our two-decade experience in dealing with the education of senior executives in the areas of management and strategy, suggests some ideas on *how* businesspeople can be effectively educated on deep ecology and sustainability.

In describing the following five possible educational actions, we try to answer the following question: "How can we make sure that busy, pragmatic, and results-oriented senior executives become better informed and more powerfully aware of deep ecology and sustainability, assuming that a lot of hurdles and resistance will be present in the process?"

Our contribution is to suggest practical ideas for immediate action in five different areas: Dialogues with Forward-Thinking Customers, Adequate Information, Benchmarking, Systemic Planning, and Individual and Collective Learning.

Dialogues with Forward-Thinking Customers

Ecologically demanding customers are good educators. Especially in these highly competitive times, when most companies are trying to become more and more "customer oriented," business executives are required to listen very carefully to their customers. And they must do so at least as attentively as they listen to their own staff, consultants, and the "community," particularly when what those people have to say is apparently disconnected from the endless demands for higher sales and profits that executives have to meet.

Today we can find, in every industry, at least a few "enlightened" customers. People who transcend the traditional business view of the world. People who have broader concerns with what is going on in the society and the planet as a whole. Those are the people who can help to educate top managers. Even the most pragmatic CEO will be sensitive to what those customers – or potential customers – have to say.

A good strategy to make this happen is to promote different sorts of dialogues – one on one or round-table format – between customers and corporate executives. First, these dialogues should include senior executives, including the CEO and the Chief Marketing Executive. Later on, staff specialists and middle management executives/teams in charge of new products, planning, and marketing/sales should be involved in the same kind of dialogue.

Needless to say, traditional surveys made by consultants or staff people are far away from the main idea here. *Direct* contact of forward-thinking customers with the company's CEO and senior managers is the key idea. Many times, top managers tend not to be motivated enough to start dialogues with customers. In this case, a good starting point would be to videotape deep interviews with ecologically aware customers. Marketing people are good at doing those kinds of interviews. Those videotaped interviews may help trigger the process, motivating the CEO to start live conversations with forward-thinking customers.

Once this process starts, the corporation as a whole will be watching what is going on in the minds of their most demanding customers (usually the "difficult" customers no one wants to deal with or even listen to). The same thing can be done with "non-customers" – former customers or potential new ones.

Listening actively to what customers have to say is a powerful learning process. Since it is already part of traditional business "wisdom," the procedure described above tends to make the insights obtained materialize quickly in the form of effective actions and changes that lead to more ecological processes, products, and management practices. The subtle change here is that instead of receiving statistically treated information on what the whole group of customers is thinking, the CEO effectively talks to forward-thinking ones (the "customers of the future").

Adequate Information

Lacking information means being ignorant. This is a self-evident truth that seemingly doesn't fully apply to the business world. Usually, in the domain of business, being "uninformed" about some things is regarded as normal if you happen to know enough about the "relevant areas." For example, it is OK to have little global culture (the arts, history, geography, "foreign culture," languages, philosophy, etc.) if you are a "financial wizard."

Traditionally, it has seemed acceptable that a senior executive have only superficial information on ecology or, even worse, be completely illiterate in that area. After all, ecology has been considered just one of those "irrelevant" issues in the "mental models" that have so far prevailed in the minds of most business people.

Now that ecology seems to have become a priority issue in every field of human activity, being ecologically literate is definitely a very desirable qualification for senior managers who hold the power to decide and make things happen in corporations. But being just literate is no longer enough. Business leaders must have "higher-level education" in ecology. It is the same rationale strategists apply in other key areas of business such as international affairs (as globalization radically changes the frontiers of the traditional business world) or telecommunications (as technology can strongly affect the strategies and the modus operandi of the organization).

Actually, ecology must be placed on a higher platform in the realm of strategic concerns of business endeavors because it is something basic, fundamental, connected to the values, mission, and purpose of the corporation. Providing high-quality products to consumers while at the same time destroying the ecological foundations of their society is, to say the least, a contradiction.

It follows that business executives should be continuously provided with adequate information on deep ecology rather than getting it in a biennial fashion or through periodical "special reports."

In the short run, we should ensure that the proper information effectively reaches all senior managers, not only through printed newsletters, clippings or memoranda, but also through personal contacts.

In our work with large corporations, we have been recommending that specific key senior managers be assigned special responsibilities regarding non-traditional issues like globalization, participation in community life, deep ecology, and the quality of life of employees and customers. Our thesis is that unless these key issues have "owners" sitting in the boardroom, they will receive only very superficial and generic attention, if any.

Of course, this doesn't mean that other key officers are not supposed to study and consider those issues while managing their areas. The main idea is that the "owner" should make sure that high-quality information is being captured and properly disseminated throughout the organization, including other senior managers, directors, and the CEO. Moreover, the "owner" is the person who carries out all the necessary steps to make things happen in the company whenever a specific piece of information is supposed to receive further attention from the corporation since it may lead to changes in policies, processes, or products.

In the long run, all the relevant information on deep ecology should be embedded in the formal management information system of the corporation. Management information systems have been transformed consistently in the last few years as corporations have been reinvented in order to cope with the demands of today's world. Quantitative data and measurements have yielded space to qualitative non-numerical information. The concept of the "balanced scorecard" clearly reflects that trend in the management information systems area.

Information on deep ecology and on how other corporations are evolving in that area should be a natural part of management information systems that include both competitors and "model companies" against which the company should benchmark itself in terms of strategies and management policies. The educational power – over the formal realm of management and the informal daily operations – of this practice is evident since it brings the concern to the heart of the company's life. A great benefit is the generation of intense dialogues on the subject in the company, leading to increased consistency in walking the talk throughout the whole organization.

As a complement, the company can create periodic information campaigns on deep ecology aiming at further raising the consciousness of employees, customers, and suppliers. But those campaigns should always be viewed as complementary media. Stronger emphasis should be placed on embedding deep ecological thinking in the daily mainstream of corporate life.

Benchmarking

Best practice educates. Pragmatic business CEOs are sensitive to real-life actions, actual examples, and results.

If we agree with the assumption that major transformation in an organization can only be possible when the main leader is actively engaged in it – is actually leading it – then the continual education of the CEO is a key factor in the cultural change necessary to bring about deep ecology consciousness in the organization.

However, CEOs are usually not easily permeable to "external" education. They tend to be averse to formal educational programs. It is our experience that even when an educational program is directed exclusively to CEOs, some of them are so sensitive that, for example, before attending a session they first check to see who the other participants are. The resistance – be it of psychological nature, an image problem, or intellectual impermeability – is usually present and should not be ignored.

The solution lies in taking the path of least resistance – using benchmarking and informal dialoguing with people they may respect, particularly other CEOs and renowned specialists who combine "advanced viewpoints" with pragmatic minds.

But a basic problem remains. How can we start the virtuous circle? How can we get the CEO involved in a benchmarking program centered on deep ecology practices? How can we get the CEO interested in talking to other CEOs and specialists about ecology?

Our experience is that those efforts should not be too narrowly focused in deep ecology and sustainability. We should keep in mind that CEOs are subject to multiple demands from a number of stakeholders – shareholders, employees, customers, suppliers, the community – and that their need for updating and education is extremely wide in scope.

A mirror approach to that multiple-demand picture leads to benchmarking programs that are systemic in their nature. It means that research aiming at discovering the best practices in the world should help CEOs get relevant information in all the fields they are interested in – not only ecology.

Fortunately, we already have companies that can be viewed as powerful benchmarks also in the area of deep ecology and sustainability (for example, Södra Cell in Sweden, Bischof and Klein in Germany, and 3M in the USA – ecologically sophisticated companies that are also showing excellent market share and bottom-line performances).

When presented to the CEO as part of a global benchmarking program, these cases will likely receive higher attention and have more credibility – more so than when presented as part of a benchmarking program "on ecology."

The same approach is recommended to round-table type programs with other CEOs and specialists. Some guest CEOs should be from companies that have best practices in quality, management of people, high technology, community services, or financial engineering. Some others should be from companies with advanced practices in deep ecology and sustainability. An interesting by-product of those gatherings (round tables could be quite informal over breakfasts or luncheons and in some cultures during "happy hours" and dinners) is that by organizing those CEO round tables the host company is also helping other CEOs to become more ecologically aware – presuming that always at least one of the members of the group is from an ecologically advanced corporation.

To start a benchmarking or round-table program with a broader scope is easier and can be suggested by anyone in the company. We already have a receptive climate in the business world for those kinds of initiatives.

Once those programs are started it is our experience that further exchange of information among the CEOs involved will quickly become a regular practice, generating accelerated evolution. Another interesting derivative phenomenon is that people from other levels of the organizations that participate in the round tables also start to exchange information and knowledge, further speeding up the process.

Systemic Planning

Planning is a powerful educational tool. Planning is thinking. Planning is creating the future through vision and orchestration of action. Planning is a process that requires a systemic perception of the corporation and of the global context in which it is inserted.

"Global context" has so far been understood as markets, the economic scenario, the social and political climate. Lately, it also includes the new connections opened by advancements in information technology and telecommunications and increased globalization. One further step in "global context" naturally takes us to deep ecology and sustainability. This is the ultimate advancement in systems thinking.

Our view here is that this ultimate step has different unfoldings. One of its dimensions is the systemic connections of the corporation to the whole – the effects on the society and on the environment of what the company does. The other dimension is its systemic effects over time, the consequences for future generations – the survival and success of the company in the long run and the well being of the society in the future.

When a company decides to engage in systemic planning, it will naturally be led to a process of thinking that takes into account deep ecology and sustainability. Our experience here is that companies are generally trapped in one or more of the following pitfalls when planning:

- they do not dare to take the ultimate step: the "traditional market" is their natural limit;
- they do not dare to go beyond the perceived possible (e.g., if they think that there is nothing they can do to improve the quality of life in society as a whole, they do not even try to think about possible solutions or contributions);
- they accept the assumption that they represent just "a drop in the ocean" and therefore are powerless;
- they accept the assumption that there is a natural limit beyond which business concerns should not go ("businesses should not enter the political realm").

Those pitfalls should be avoided. They are assumptions that have to be overcome if the corporation is to go beyond the mere concern for short-term survival and effectively create its future in a better world.

Systemic planning helps to overcome those traps and negative assumptions, educating everyone involved with it – from the CEO to the plant worker.

Systemic planning necessarily opens up possibilities for the achievement of ideal futures. Nothing is impossible when we consider the outstanding achievement potential of an aligned society. We can create a better society if we all decide to and have the political intention to do so. If that can be envisioned through systemic thinking and vision, its achievement is just a matter of creativity and joint effort.

Systemic planning opens the minds of senior executives to the interdependence of everything in the world, thereby calling their attention to the importance of deep ecology and the concept of sustainability. It also shows a new range of possibilities for the future through full cooperation among all segments of society. It helps create a new vision of the possible for business and for the society.

In the pragmatic business world we usually have few opportunities for deep thinking in the midst of daily affairs. But planning is already an accepted institution in most corporations. When systemic planning displaces guesswork and mere budget-building processes it becomes an outstandingly valuable non-threatening educational tool for senior executives. Systemic planning naturally leads all of us to a more ecological way of thinking.

Individual and Collective Learning

Learning is much more than being educated. Learning implies something that comes from the inside of the person. "Being educated" implies that the learning is coming from the outside (if the paradigm is the old-fashioned way of educating top-down, from the one who knows and has the right answers to the ones who don't have the knowledge and don't know the "correct answers").

There is a lot to be done both in the areas of individual and collective learning and in education in the new paradigm (educators and learners evolving together, educators as catalysts of learning). Although ecological awareness should come up more from daily activities and not just from formal courses, we should not place formal education on a secondary level.

In our view, a lot can be achieved in the area of ecological education through business schools, in-house courses and institutional programs geared to foster self-learning and collective learning.

Our post-graduate course for experienced business executives has been a pioneering program in Brazil in preparing senior managers in systems thinking focused on leadership/top management issues. Details of this program as related to ecological principles are described in the insert at the end of this chapter.

By raising the level of awareness of its participants, the program naturally leads to deep ecology and sustainability values. The program covers a broad set of issues related to modern management, balancing highly conceptual questions with very pragmatic ideas for action allowing the participants to be connected to their daily experiences. But every topic covered in the program is probed in terms of basic human values and the importance of raising the level of consciousness.

The outcome of the approach is a fundamental transformation of the participants' view of life, work, and the community. As one of the participants put it: "the course is a synthesis of something broader ... as we work the 12 competencies, we naturally go beyond the process of managing business concerns: it is a deep reflection about the best we can do for humankind ... about our legacy for the society as a whole ..."

Business schools in general can help achieve a lot in the short run through executive development programs aligned to systems thinking and broad ecological principles. As business schools also play a fundamental role in developing future senior managers, their contribution to the development of a higher ecological awareness cannot be neglected. Changes currently being introduced in the schools' curricula can have tremendous positive impact in the medium/long run. For example, the J. L. Kellogg Graduate School of Management at Northwestern University in the U.S. added a course on environmental issues for business to its MBA program. This is an excellent start. The hope is that other business schools will follow the trend, adding courses in deep ecology and sustainable development.

However, in our view, changes in business schools should go beyond that. The ideas and values of ecology and sustainability should be present in every course covered by the program. In finance, the issue of quantitative/qualitative returns will bring ecological concerns into the right perspective; in marketing, the issue of ethics and changing values of the customers will raise the awareness of the students, etc.

As to the in-house courses, the principles are similar to the ones applied to business schools. Almost every training program under way in corporations may have to be changed to reflect the new values of deep ecology and sustainability.

Our experience here is that senior managers will be getting themselves more and more involved in coaching and educating new managers, rather than using their time to control and to supervise. As senior people start to play the role of coaches, an interesting phenomenon will tend to occur: they will absorb and internalize more deeply the "content and values" of what they teach. In short, they will learn a lot as they "teach."

Also, the results of the training process – when senior people are the facilitators of the programs – will tend to be quite more significant, as participants feel that the company has better conditions to actually walk the talk. Needless to say, those in-house programs have to be consistent with what the company is actually achieving in the area of ecology and sustainability.

As to other institutional programs, two areas should be emphasized. The first is the climate for self-development and continuous evolution. As the company makes every possible learning tool (including computer simulators in systems thinking) available to everyone and motivates people to look for self-development, the organization will tend to build quickly the necessary critical mass for the overall evolution to a higher level of awareness in ecology and sustainability.

The second area is the incentive for collective learning. As "people who know" feel that they are responsible for disseminating their "know-how" to others (a company value to be cultivated) "communities of learning" will tend to proliferate throughout the organization. Since the objective of these communities is everyone's professional and personal evolution, the subject of ethics, values, and consciousness will come up naturally, later evolving towards the issues of ecology and sustainability.

Professors, professional trainers, leaders as coaches, and consultants are "multipliers" and "opinion makers." As we focus on the education of business executives in the area of ecology and sustainability, that group should receive special attention in terms of alignment of values, systemic mindsetting, and "non-threatening" communication approaches.

Also, in the medium to long run, as ecological values become "official" within the corporations, human resources systems will have to be thoroughly adjusted to them. For example, the evaluation and reward systems will have to be aligned to new values adopted by the organization. Likewise, overall management policies and systems will tend to be transformed accordingly.

Conclusions

In this chapter, we shared some of our ideas and experiences in management education geared to deep ecology and sustainability. They represent above all a metaphor about the balance between conceptual thinking and pragmatic action.

Business concerns are rapidly becoming the most powerful institution of the planet. They have a tremendous power to help create a considerably better or worse world. And most of that power does not come from their financial or technological resources. It stems from the people. People who have been trained to be productive as a group. People trained to make things happen.

Nonetheless, paradoxically, the business world still hesitates in fully using its strength to build a better world. A world with a higher quality of life for everyone on the planet.

Businesspeople are hesitant because they are still bound to a lower level of consciousness. A level where the prevailing assumption is the "survival of the fittest" in a world of limited resources.

As we quickly approach a new world where resources are no longer the leverage factor for change, where values, ideas, knowledge, and human talent are the new key factors of "success," we also become conscious of the new possibilities open for the human being. The "impossible" is becoming possible.

The "possible impossible" seems to be the realm of the people who dare to act. The ones that courageously take the first steps towards their ideals, their dream.

A good story that illustrates that point is the case of Mrs. Jocélia Santos de Souza, a young wife of a construction worker living in a very poor neighborhood of São Paulo, Brazil. Noticing that many small children in the region did not have anything to eat because both parents were at work the whole day, she decided to offer lunch for three children who were playing with her own children. The following day she had six children coming for lunch. And they kept coming: 10, 20, 50. As the group got larger, help from neighbors naturally started to come. Today, she is providing almost one thousand meals every day and keeps creating new projects to help those children develop a decent future for themselves through better education and better work opportunities.

The fundamental question that is in the heart of that story is: What would have happened to her 'project' if she – before offering the first three meals – had decided to make a "feasibility study," as we are used to doing in the business world? Would she have started it?

Businesspeople seem to be still hesitant, spending their time with unending feasibility studies on "ecology projects." This is a time for action. For first steps. Ideas are great but they must be quickly followed by courageous action.

This is a time for global action. As globalization is definitely something beyond a mere theory, and as high technology actualizes, for the first time in history, the idea of humanity, we seem to have today all the necessary conditions to create a better world for all.

It is time to act. And as we go in the right direction, unexpected doors will be open, making the apparently "impossible" a reality.

That certainly is not a typical business assumption. It is an assumption that transcends the traditional business realm.

Educating for deep ecology and sustainability goes beyond the education of minds. Ultimately, it leads to the evolution of the spirit.

Amana-Key's Systemic Executive Development Program

The emergent understanding of business organizations as living organisms in permanent change stresses the need for a new breed of managers. This new manager faces novel roles beyond the traditional technical approach to business. Totally new competencies are required to manage a corporation under the new vision in a world quite different from the past. Based on those assumptions, the Amana-Key Group created in 1991 an innovative systemic executive development program. The program is an educational process in which the new roles of managers are intertwined with principles of systems thinking to evoke ways to lead business towards an unprecedented future. Amana-Key's program, offered only to experienced executives and focused on top management issues, is based on twelve key roles of the new business leader. Eight of these roles are naturally interwoven with principles of deep ecology. Those eight roles are:

The Executive as a Statesman (The Principle of Interdependence)
The performance of the corporation's role in the community implies the understanding and application of the principle of interdependence. When "corporate citizenship" is perceived as an overarching value, executives apprehend how interconnected we all are and how we influence the biopolitical and social fabric of the whole.

The Executive as a Strategist (The Principle of Flexibility)
The "new strategy" draws on concepts such as strategic intent, and resources leverage. These ideas trigger non-linear processes that require leaders to know the fluctuations that their organizations can cope with. When managers realize the need for higher levels of flexibility they re-evaluate their beliefs and tend to become more aligned to an ecological, more natural "style" of creating the future.

The Executive as a Change Agent (The Principle of Ecological Cycles)
The permanent interchange of matter and energy among the elements of an ecosystem becomes evident in a corporation that looks at itself as a living organism. Under this perspective, innovation becomes "biological," i.e., naturally accepted as part of a dynamic flow of ideas, resources, and people who make things happen.

The Executive as an Architect of Processes and Networks (The Principle of Partnership)
The emerging idea of organizations as "communities of learning" is an outcome of the principle of partnership. More and more managers realize that they, customers, suppliers, the community, and the eco-social environment are all interconnected in a network of cooperative relationships.

The Executive as a Negotiator (The Principle of Diversity)
Mastering the skills to deal with the complexity of human interactions and reconcile divergent interests leads us to recognize that the richness of a group of people (or ecosystem) depends on its diversity. To be a negotiator the manager has to learn to respect the uniqueness of each living organism and find out how to deal with diversity.

The Executive as an Educator (The Principle of Co-Evolution)
The principle of co-evolution calls for creative interchange and adaptability. The executive as an educator draws on those qualities to deploy the capabilities that will transform the company into a learning organization. People, then, become the main value of the organization as the evolution of products and technologies tends to be-

come a natural consequence of the learning processes and the optimal unfolding of the group's full potentials.

The Executive as a Living Example (The Principle of Energy Flow)

The "solar energy" within an organization is generated by quality of the flow of actions of its people. To become a living example of this principle the manager has to shift from "knowledge" to "wisdom" and walk the talk. That behavior in itself opens the "flow of energy" throughout the organization and keeps the way to it in a sound state of "dynamic equilibrium."

The Executive as a Cultivator of Values (The Principle of Sustainability)

The effective practice of universal values in the organization is consistent with the development of an "overall culture" compatible with the present and future needs of the planet. That culture is organically fostered by the executive that always takes into account the welfare of the whole today and tomorrow. This is the essence of sustainability that arises when the thoughtful manager sees himself/herself and the company as part of an indivisible and integrated whole.

5

Assessing Corporate Environmental Performance

Luis L. Martins, Charles J. Fombrun, and Alice Tepper Marlin*

José Lutzenberger and Oscar Motomura both emphasized in previous chapters that access to fast and reliable environmental data is crucial for designing strategies for ecological sustainability. This recognition is spreading rapidly in today's business world. The most influential daily paper in business is the Financial Times *of London. Ten years ago there was no page on the environment in the* Times, *but when the last appointment for editor in chief was considered, Francis Cairncross, a leading environmental writer, was seriously considered for this top job. And when the Worldwatch Institute published the latest version of its* Vital Signs *last September, the* Financial Times *gave it front-page attention. Not only that, the ordering information for the book was placed right there as well.*

The business media are realizing that there is an urgent need for providing corporate executives with relevant environmental data. As the financial media, both print and electronic, search for new services, environmental data provision is becoming one of the hottest areas of development. Reuters, the undisputed leader in electronic financial data and news, has established a task force to design a framework for on-line information on environmental performance of publicly traded companies. Based in the UK, Reuters serves mainly European customers and, as Japanese and American companies listed on European stock exchanges have noted, European investors are highly conscious of environmental performance.

When Mitsubishi organized a road show in 1990 in preparation for

*This chapter has benefited from the helpful comments of Sean Morton.

its entry into the Paris and London stock exchanges, the president of this large trading and industrial group had prepared carefully for all imaginable questions. However, in previous years, Mitsubishi had been widely criticized by NGOs for its environmentally destructive forestry practices in the Southern Hemisphere, and the company's president was shocked about the detailed knowledge of that critique among institutional investors who kept asking him extremely tough questions. For a moment he even thought he had entered the wrong room and was facing a panel of activists from Greenpeace and the Rainforest Action Network.

With increasing interest in environmental information by institutional investors there is increasing demand for data on corporate environmental performance. To be sure, most of this information is of a qualitative nature, unlike data on sales, cost price structure, return on investment, and the like. This makes the job for the data providers more difficult, since the information needs to be timely and correct even though it is always subject to interpretation.

However, we need to remember that value judgments are always qualitative. As more data on environmental performance become available, potential investors may change their mind on the present value of a company. If its environmental performance is outstanding, the company is bound to gain from this recognition, increase its sales, expand its profit margins, generate higher customer satisfaction, and create customer loyalty. On the other hand, if the environmental data reveal that the company is lagging behind its competitors and only meets the minimum environmental standards, present shareholders may decide that the risks involved are too high and may sell, driving the stock price down.

Traditional information providers such as Reuters, Quick, Telerate, and Quotron, as well as Dunn and Bradstreet, are important sources of environmental information. However, over the next few years much more information will become available over the informal electronic networks emerging on the Internet. For example, Econet offers a review of all companies currently boycotted because of their shortcomings in environmental or social performance.

In the past these boycotts had very little international exposure, but through today's Internet, data on environmental performance can be made available globally almost instantaneously. As the Internet expands, business will have to become aware of the fact that soon ten times more people will be connected to it than to Reuters, Quick, Telerate, and Quotron combined. This will represent the kind of free in-

formation postulated by Adam Smith as a precondition to a perfectly functioning market. Businesses will then either have to tap into this network to know what the world thinks about them, or risk exposure to a world opinion detrimental to them.

Making environmental data available is one thing; producing reliable data is something else. Rating the environmental performance of corporations is a complex task that has been developed to a high degree in the United States by organizations like the Council on Economic Priorities. The organization's founder, Alice Tepper Marlin, and her colleagues Charles Fombrun and Luis Martins of the Stern School of Business in New York City survey the criteria for environmental assessment, the ways in which awards are given, ratings are established, and corporate shortcomings in environmental responsibility are spotlighted. They show how these techniques combine both to influence consumer buying behavior and to help corporations achieve more satisfactory environmental performance.

Introduction

Although environmental organizations in the United States often possess impressive technical expertise, they tend to focus on individual dramatic issues of pollution or toxic hazards rather than on broader questions of how corporate activities impact the natural world. Systematic assessment of corporate environmental performance has been pioneered by the Council on Economic Priorities as part of its wider assessments of corporate "citizenship." CEP's ratings in the category of "environmental stewardship" depend on grading such factors as compliance with federal and local laws, product design and packaging, energy efficiency, and minimization of toxic releases. The resulting ratings are widely publicized, as we will explain below, and influence both consumer and management behavior.

CEP has accumulated a large data bank enabling it to make objective comparisons among companies. A top-rated company on the environment is one that has relatively low and declining toxic releases, adjusted for the size of the company. It is one that has made achieving environmental goals an integral part of management performance review and compensation systems. It discloses specific goals, timetables, and progress. Often, top-rated manufacturers participate in voluntary Environmental Protection Agency programs on toxic release reduction or energy efficiency.

CEP also rates companies on building-design features like energy sources, energy efficiency of lighting, use of sustainably harvested timber, user-friendly provisions for collecting returnable and recyclable materials, and adoption of CFC substitutes in refrigeration. Supermarkets get credit for sizable offerings of organic produce and minimal packaging on private labels. Companies that adopt "green" specifications of products, components, or services and communicate them to vendors and contractors are rewarded. Ratings also credit environmental shelf-labeling derived from government or other independent sources – Swedish supermarkets are especially outstanding at this.

Since environmental stewardship is the most complex and data-rich criterion on which CEP rates corporations, it publishes 20–90 page reports detailing corporate environmental programs and performance. Based on public information as well as company reports, these often serve corporations as the equivalent of paid outside consultant reports and provide the basis for ongoing environmental improvement programs. CEP's methods are now being employed by sister organizations in Britain (New Consumer), Germany (IMUG), and Japan (Asahi Shimbun). Although CEP is not hesitant to name low-performing companies in its Campaign for Cleaner Corporations, its aim is to motivate such companies to improve their performance and secure credit for genuine responsiveness in future ratings, and it can point to some success in this direction.

In the United States, some environmental organizations such as the Environmental Defense Fund and the Natural Resources Defense Council have been concentrating attention on specific companies with the aim of decreasing their environmental impacts. These efforts, based on expertise rivalling and in some areas surpassing that of the companies themselves, have had profound effects. The EDF, through a long-standing program that was often sharply adversarial, brought about fundamental changes in the investment policies of Pacific Gas & Electric (the country's largest investor-owned utility). In a contrasting cooperative vein, NRDC has engaged in an extensive (and unpaid) consultantship with McDonald's which has led to changes in practically every aspect of that company's fast-food operation.

Environmental Awards

Environmental awards have become increasingly popular tools in the U.S. for recognizing companies that try to promote energy efficiency and minimize pollution. Sponsors hope that awards will encourage other companies to imitate them, and will thereby foster greater ecological awareness and interest in questions of global sustainability.

There are now many environmental awards. Some are backed by government agencies, some are given by watchdog groups, others are sponsored by companies themselves. Two of the more prestigious awards are the *Gold Medal for International Corporate Achievement*, and the *Global 500 Roll of Honour for Environmental Achievement.*

- The *Gold Medal* Award honors industrial companies that have shown outstanding, sustained, and well-implemented environmental management policies in their international operations. In the late 1980s, the Award was repeatedly singled out by U.S. President George Bush, adding to its visibility.
- The *Global 500* is sponsored by the United Nations Environmental Program. Nominations are made by third parties and awards are given in 27 areas of environmental accomplishment. The awards identify individuals and NGOs, and a few companies, that have demonstrated sustainable development practices; that have mobilized public attention and support, or taken action toward solving an environmental protection issue; or that have contributed significantly to intellectual, scientific, or theoretical approaches to environmental concerns.

Other environmental awards given in the U.S. include:

- *The DuPont/Conoco Environmental Leadership Award:* Based on nominations from customers of DuPont or Conoco Mining Services, companies with mining operations in North America are assessed on their success in reclaiming mines, protecting land-use and water quality, and in local environmental leadership.
- *The Edison Award for Environmental Achievement:* Sponsored by the American Marketing Association, the award champions American companies whose commercial products contribute significantly to source reduction.
- *The Environmental Achievement Award:* Given to companies whose environmental projects exceed regulatory requirements and who develop creative and innovative solutions with proven economic and environmental benefits. The award is sponsored by the National Wildlife Federation's Corporate Conservation Council.
- *The Safety Award for Excellence (SAFE):* Targets oil companies that achieve the highest levels of safety and environmental compliance in U.S. off-shore drilling operations. Nominees are picked from inspection reports, and the award is sponsored by the Minerals Management Service of the U.S. Department of the Interior.

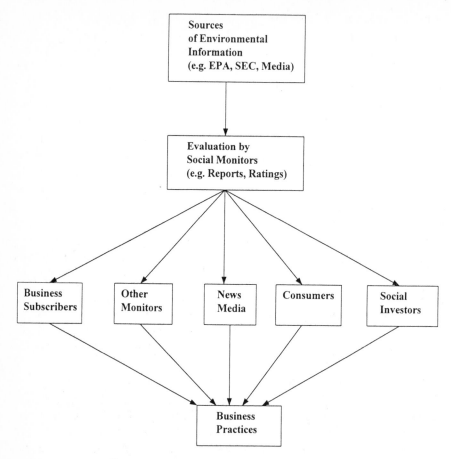

Fig. 1 **Assessing Environmental Performance**

- *Searching for Success National Environmental Achievement Award:* Sponsored by the not-for-profit group RENEW America, awards are made in twenty environmental categories to individuals, community groups, schools, companies, or government agencies with outstanding environmental programs.
- *America's Corporate Conscience Awards:* Sponsored by the Council on Economic Priorities, a non-profit public policy research organization based in New York, a group of both small and large companies are recognized annually for their achievements in five categories of social and environmental responsiveness.

Despite their apparent diversity, all of these awards, in fact, rely on common sources of information about firms and their environmental performance. In this chapter, we review:

- the principal *sources* of environmental information in the U.S.,
- the *process through which environmental information gets conveyed to outside observers, and*
- the *effects* that these environmental data have on the business practices of U.S. firms.

We conclude with a brief discussion of future prospects for improving corporate environmental performance. Figure 1 sketches the basic framework of the chapter.

Assessing Environmental Performance

Despite an apparent diversity of awards and sponsors, there are remarkably few *credible, independent, or objective* sources of information about firms' environmental performance. The two principal sources of data in the U.S. are:

- Regulatory Agencies
- Business Media and Mass Media

Several agencies of the U.S. government have been empowered by legislation to collect and disseminate information about the environmental performance of firms. The agencies are part of a regulatory web in the U.S. that now requires firms to compile and report on a regular basis certain key measures that demonstrate the impact of these firms' operations on the environment. These government agencies are responsible for maintaining the data in useable form. The two key agencies in the regulatory web are the Environmental Protection Agency (EPA) and the Securities and Exchange Commission (SEC). The quality and availability of their data varies.

Among the most visible of databases is the *Toxic Release Inventory* (TRI) created as part of the U.S. Congress's Emergency Planning and Community Right-to-Know Act, also known as Title III of the Superfund Amendments and Reauthorization Act (SARA). Enacted in 1986, the TRI documents information on the types and amounts of toxic materials released by manufacturing units. The chemicals listed in the TRI range from mildly toxic to highly toxic. Since its inception, however, the list has changed as chemicals that were originally judged toxic have been removed from the list while others that were not on the original list but were subsequently found to be toxic were added. The TRI now covers 368 individual toxins and 20 chemical categories.

The information contained in the TRI is reported by the companies themselves. Facilities that manufacture, import, or process more than 50,000 pounds – or use more than 10,000 pounds – of toxic chemicals are required to report to the EPA the amount of those chemicals that were either released into the environment or sent for off-site treatment or disposal. Only since 1991 have companies been required to report chemicals sent to *off-site* facilities for recycling or reuse.

TRI data, as currently reported, have several drawbacks. First, they cover only about 0.5% of the approximately 60,000 registered chemicals. Second, many of the companies' TRI reports are based on *estimated* releases and not on definitive monitoring. Third, the list of chemicals in the TRI and reporting format are constantly updated, making year-to-year and firm-to-firm comparisons difficult. Despite these drawbacks, however, the availability of TRI data has meant a quantum leap forward in our ability to apprehend the impact that businesses have on the environment. The EPA is currently working on some of the drawbacks of the TRI and will hopefully develop a more inclusive and stable listing of toxic chemicals.

Several other databases on environmental issues are compiled by agencies of the U.S. government and made available to the public. The Aerometric Information Retrieval System (AIRS) database records companies' levels of air permit compliance, and is maintained by the EPA. The Occupational Safety and Health Administration (OSHA) of the U.S. Department of Labor collects and summarizes information on various worker safety and health related violations by companies. Information is available on the number of violations, the breakdown of types of violations, and the fines remitted as a consequence of OSHA violations.

The Sites Enforcement Tracking System of the EPA lists the number of federal Superfund sites at which a company has been identified by the EPA as a potentially responsible party. The Superfund is a pool of money collected from a tax on the chemical and petroleum industries created under the Comprehensive Environmental Response, Compensation, and Liability Act (CERCLA) which was passed by the U.S. Congress in 1980. Each Superfund expends money to "clean up" abandoned or uncontrolled hazardous waste sites. Before any clean-up takes place, however, a legally complex and expensive process seeks to determine responsible firms through careful historical examination; often lengthy legal proceedings are involved.

Securities regulation creates another key source of information on corporate environmental performance. Under modifications to the U.S. Securities and Exchange (SEC) Acts of 1933 and 1934, companies are required to declare "the material effects that compliance with environmental law may have upon capital expenditures" and to provide shareholders with dollar estimates of any other impacts on capital expenditures that might result from environmental compliance. They therefore require that firms provide investors with a rough estimate of the costs that were incurred or are expected as a consequence of a company's impact on the environment. Companies provide these data in many SEC information filings.

A problem arises, however. Although the new SEC reporting requirements provide easy access to cost estimates of environmental responsiveness, the estimates themselves are not necessarily reliable. For one, remediation costs are difficult to quantify. Moreover, no clear definitions of terms such as "compliance costs" exists, so that each company develops its own definition – and therefore its own idiosyncratic estimates – of what compliance costs will be.

Besides regulatory agencies, the news media are the only other key source of independent information on companies' environmental performance. News reports are particularly useful in gathering and disseminating information about regional events. Whereas a company's overall environmental record might show good environmental performance, local news from a small community in which the company operates a manufacturing plant might tell a very different story. In recent years, the growing availability of large computerized databases that enable rapid search of diverse news media has significantly increased the power of even small town newspapers to reach a wider audience.

Despite the growing availability of information on firms' environmental performance, however, it remains true that most of the data are still widely dispersed and not easily accessed. Often they are buried in larger reports, or are presented in a format that requires aggregation, making it time consuming to collect and ambiguous to interpret them. To overcome these limitations, a number of non-governmental organizations have developed over the years that play a pivotal role in facilitating collection and dissemination of environmental data. They include two principal types of groups:
- Social Monitors
- Corporate Coalitions

Both of these groups draw on common government and media

sources for information about companies' environmental performance. They play a key role in summarizing and diffusing interpretations about firms to other observers.

Diffusing Environmental Information

Various social monitors dedicate themselves to gathering and disseminating environmental information on companies. Their primary purpose is to pull together from diverse sources information about firms' environmental performance. They act as a clearinghouse of sorts and make environmental information more readily accessible to consumers.

Social monitors differ in their information sources. Many rely exclusively on government data. Their reports tend to address customers interested in assessing environmental liabilities at a particular site. Of these social monitors, the following are among the more prominent:

- *Environmental Data Sources, Inc.:* A Connecticut firm that offers extensive searches of over 300 government databases.
- *Vista:* A company headquartered in California that provides environmental risk assessment based on a search of over 500 government databases.
- Others include: *Dun & Bradstreet in* New Providence, New Jersey; *Environmental Risk Information and Imaging Services* in Alexandria, Virginia; and *Agency Information Consultants, Inc,* in Austin, Texas.

A second group of social monitors relies not only on government data but on primary research to develop environmental profiles of companies. *Kinder, Lydenberg, Domini & Co., Inc.,* for instance, is based in Cambridge, Massachusetts and sells corporate profiles and a database of ratings on some 750 companies that are among the largest in the U.S. Their Domini 400 Social Index has gained visibility as a tool for monitoring the profitability of investments in socially responsible companies. The *Investor Responsibility Research Center* (IRRC) is a Washington D.C. not-for-profit group that provides short reports on government compliance data on all the S&P 500 firms. Finally, the *Council on Economic Priorities* (CEP) is a research organization based in New York that provides information about the social and environmental records of corporations, with the goal of influencing their "economic vote."

Social Monitors: The Case of CEP

Although there are a growing number of social monitors who issue ratings of companies, we focus here on those of the Council on Economic Priorities (CEP) because of the breadth of their offerings as well as their availability in a variety of formats, including books, disks, reports, and lists. CEP's best-selling books aim to make consumers more socially and environmentally conscious. They include the organization's annual *Shopping for a Better World* (Ballantine Books 1990–1993; Sierra Club Books, 1994) and *The Better World Investment Guide* (Prentice-Hall). Both books provide user-friendly information on how corporations rate on various social and environmental performance criteria.

Besides publishing occasional books, CEP also regularly circulates 20–90 page reports on the environmental policies and practices of specific corporations. The reports are relatively unique in that they compare each company to others in the industry on a variety of criteria. Another service provides interested customers with more concise quarterly summaries of the social and environmental records of approximately 700 U.S. and international corporations.

Every year, CEP also conducts some more focused campaigns. The annual "America's Corporate Conscience Awards" recognizes firms whose policies and practices indicate abiding concern for social and environmental responsibility. The "Campaign for Cleaner Corporations" identifies some of the U.S.'s *worst* environmental performers relative to their industry peers. The campaign invokes participation from a wide range of consumer, environmental, civic, and investor organizations in a collective effort to improve corporate environmental policies and practices.

Critical to preparing these digests of environmental information are systematic procedures for collecting, analyzing, and presenting information. CEP relies on information gathered, not only from the EPA, OSHA, the SEC, and the regional and national media, but from other government publications, legal databases, business and environmental organizations, and corporations themselves. Most of the data are summarized in absolute terms as well as in comparative form to industry rivals.

Environmental ratings of companies are based on industry questionnaires that are prepared by CEP staff with help from industry and environmental experts. Companies provide self-reported information about their environmental policies and practices. Often the data reveal valuable insights that would not otherwise be available from secondary sources. They also provide judges with an insider's view, and so a more complete profile of a company's environmental posture.

Corporate information is combined with information gathered from secondary sources, including government databases, computerized searches of newspapers, periodicals, and other publications, internal CEP files, news clippings, company literature, annual reports, 10-K filings, proxy statements, and other SEC documents. All data are later reviewed and entered into an environmental ratings template. Each subcategory of environmental ratings is given a relative weight based on expert input from CEP's advisors. The subcategories are rated individually based on the ratings template. Finally, through a systematic computation process, an overall rating of the company is developed and communicated to both the company and to advisors, who review the rating and identify areas for clarification, more information or discrepancies. Any new information acquired in the process is input into the rating template and a new rating computed for each subcategory. The subcategories are then recombined to obtain a revised overall rating.

In most of its work, CEP relies on panels of judges to determine which firms to nominate for awards or to highlight on lists. Judges are invariably comprised of prominent experts from the relevant disciplines. Nominated firms are contacted for additional information, based on which the panels determine which companies to include and decide the lists and the winners to announce publicly.

Monitoring Networks

Besides social monitors, a number of groups have coalesced into networks to share environmental information, communicate best practices, create standards of environmental reporting, or disseminate reports to consumers. Two of these are among the more visible: The Coalition for Environmentally Responsible Economies (CERES) and the Public Environmental Reporting Initiative (PERI).

CERES is a not-for-profit membership organization comprised of leading social investment professionals, environmental groups, religious organizations, public pension trustees, and public interest groups. The network was launched in 1989, and focuses on the various ways investors can help to implement environmentally and financially sound investment policies. In 1993, the coalition claimed

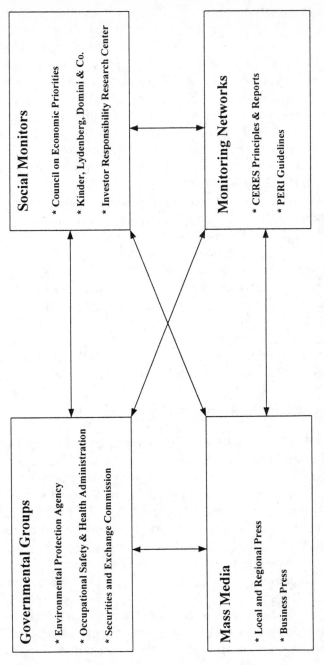

Fig. 2 **Monitoring Environmental Performance**

to speak for more than 10 million people and to represent over $150 billion in invested assets. The CERES Principles are a ten-point environmental ethic that endorsing companies pledge to follow by monitoring and improving their results on protecting the biosphere; exploring sustainable use of natural resources; reducing waste; conserving energy; enhancing product and service safety; restoring the environment; and informing the public. Endorsing companies back up these pledges with concrete information and public revelation in the annual CERES Report. Like some other social monitors, CERES Reports provide consumers with capsule summaries and longer reports of voluntarily disclosed corporate information. The reports do not assign relative rankings to endorsing companies.

The PERI Guidelines were developed by a coalition of companies from different industry sectors. The group researched how various social monitors like CEP and IRRC assessed companies and summarized their findings as guidelines for environmental reporting. The Guidelines are intended to encourage other companies to move voluntarily towards improving their environmental performance. The group does not in and of itself create reports; rather, it describes the kind of information a company should provide to consumers in order to demonstrate environmental responsiveness.

Figure 2 summarizes the major groups involved in monitoring companies and their environmental performance.

Consumers of Environmental Information

Not all consumers of environmental information are the same. For instance, although most reports are available to all interested parties for a fee, each is generally aimed at a specific audience. In-depth reports on corporate environmental performance are generally of particular interest to grassroots environmentalists, law firms specializing in environmental issues, large nonprofit groups such as the World Wildlife Fund, Sierra Club, and Greenpeace, as well as research organizations, lobbying groups, investment managers, institutional investors, environmental engineers, educators, environmental regulators such as the EPA, state-level Departments of Environmental Protection, and corporations themselves. Shorter reports tend to target socially-screened mutual funds, foundations, investment managers, and stock brokers who want to direct their investment dollars toward companies that are socially and environmentally responsible. CEP's best-selling guidebook *Shopping for a Better World* is aimed at consumers of corporations' products. It evaluates over 2,000 products of some 191 major companies with the objective of influencing consumers' purchases and, ultimately, corporate social and environmental performance.

The news media are both consumers of the environmental reports of social monitors and active disseminators. Reports of social monitors are often used by reporters for newspapers and magazines – thereby magnifying the reach and impact of a social monitor on the public and, indirectly, on firms. The news media actually extends the reach of a social monitor to consumers who are not subscribers to its products. News reports based on a social monitor's reports or ratings also affect other groups that routinely monitor the news.

As varied as are the consumers of environmental information published by social monitors, so too are the uses to which that information is put. Business subscribers often use the reports of social monitors to read the environmental performance of their industry and to identify "best practices" to model. They often use those same reports to promote their own environmental performance.

Often competing social monitors will rely on each other's reports to inform their own campaigns and programs. The reports not only provide information on companies' environmental performances, but also are often pointers to sources of information that other social monitors might explore further. The in-depth reports of some social monitors also prove useful to small regional environmental groups looking for information on a company's local facilities. Government agencies and offices also use these reports as an added check on the accuracy of a company's environmental claims.

Many social investors, pension fund managers, and institutional investors find the information compiled by social monitors to be valuable in selecting investments or voting on proxies. Attorneys, environmental engineers, financial accountants, and public relations professionals use the in-depth reports of social monitors for a quick read on a company's environmental performance, saving themselves the enormous time and effort that would be required to put together a comprehensive profile of the firm. Educators and students use them as reading material in courses and as data for research projects. Many individual consumers rely on the guidelines of social monitors to help them choose what products to buy, which companies to invest in, and which companies to work for.

Impacting Business Practices

Environmental information disseminated by social and environmental monitors impacts corporate environmental practices in a number of ways. Some of the impacts are direct while others operate indirectly through a diffuse network of individuals and organizations. Often individuals in companies, even high officials, are not aware of their own environmental record. Often they are also unaware of what their competitors are doing, and how they compare to their competitors. Social monitors help companies directly to improve their environmental performance by providing subscribers with environmental digests and profiles that enable them to make decisions about their own environmental policies and practices. For these consumers, the information serves both as a report card of their own standing on environmental issues, as well as a benchmark against other companies which they want to emulate or surpass.

When a social monitor lists a company among the worst environmental performers in its industry, the group generally provides the company with recommendations for remedial action. At CEP, for instance, each company is invited to meet with the ratings staff and work out solutions to its environmental problems. The judges communicate to the company the various things it needs to do in order to demonstrate an improved environmental record. CEP therefore directly influences corporate decision makers, and thereby impacts corporate environmental practices.

Much of the advice provided to a firm comes from the expertise of experienced advisors, but it is enhanced by knowledge that other companies in the company's industry have developed and are using in their own environmental practices. In this way, social monitors also act as an industry-level disseminator of information about environmental best-practices.

Companies prefer to avoid bad publicity and are generally quick to react to news coverage that contains environmental information on their companies. News reports will therefore typically prompt firms to initiate public relations efforts as well as to take a closer look at their environmental practices – if only to avoid bad press in the future. The news media therefore play a key role in indirectly impacting business practices. Media reports also influence consumers, who react either by mail and phone campaigns to offending firms or by changing their buying patterns.

Social investors also rely on information from social monitors.

They use environmental data to channel their investment dollars and vote their proxies. By reacting to environmental information, they send a message to offending companies about their environmental practices. As a result, environmental information compiled and disseminated by social monitors can also indirectly influence the firm's environmental practices.

In this way, then, social monitors play a key role in collecting and disseminating environmental information, and so stand to affect business practices. Despite these developments, however, much work remains to be done if we are to create a truly responsive and responsible business sector. We suggest some avenues to pursue.

Future Improvements

Two questions come to mind when thinking about future prospects for improving the environmental performance of firms and achieving global sustainability:
• How might we improve on data currently *available*?
• How might we improve on information *dissemination*?

Improving Data Availability

Impressive improvements have been made in data availability about U.S. firms in the last few years. Despite regulatory initiatives and the voluntary disclosure standards embodied in the CERES Principles and the PERI Guidelines, problems of standardization remain, making comparability difficult from year to year and from company to company. Stronger disclosure rules could help rectify these problems.

Without a doubt, corporate participation in voluntary disclosure programs helps. However, disclosure rules now require companies to estimate only the *legal* costs of compliance, such as those incurred in complying with regulations and paying fines for regulatory violations. Yet many of the real costs associated with poor environmental performance involve the loss of "reputational capital" that stems from negative publicity. Lowered market values of public companies are surrogate measures of the implicit costs of non-compliance that could be estimated and disclosed.

Finally, good environmental performance affords solid benefits, not only to those who live near unsound facilities, but to a company's consumers and other constituencies. It would be useful to balance the disclosure equation with estimates not only of hidden costs, but of hidden benefits. Estimating these benefits could be an attractive carrot with which to attract non-performing firms.

Improving Data Dissemination

There may be ways to heighten cooperation among existing government agencies, NGOs, and others actively disseminating environmental information. As environmental awards, ratings, and reports proliferate, we need closer coordination among evaluating institutions to produce consistent reports. At a minimum, a closer alliance between social monitors would reduce the kinds of contradictory assessments that invariably damage the credibility and reputation of *all* environmental monitors.

In an era of rapidly evolving communications media, new methods could also be developed to tap, summarize, and disseminate environmental information. Most social monitors rely on labor intensive methods to distill environmental information and could doubtless benefit from more sophisticated access to computerized technologies for information manipulation. Here, too, we see significant potential for cooperative benefits in shared networks among social monitors to minimize duplication of effort.

Finally, we have dealt in this chapter exclusively with the situation in the U.S. Given the relative success of social monitors like CEP in the U.S., we foresee clear benefits from developing a web of such organizations worldwide. Only in this way might we improve environmental performance in the *global* village to which we all belong.

6

Media, Community, and Business

Eric Utne

When we planned to include a chapter on the role of the media in steering business toward sustainability, we had no idea what the conclusions of this chapter would be. First of all, we asked ourselves, what do we mean by "the media"? Should we limit ourselves to the mass media – the television networks and leading mass-circulation newspapers and magazines – or should we include the "alternative press" as a counterpoint to the views of the establishment? Should we perhaps focus on the business press? What about the independent local radio stations, which tend to be grassroots operations but are often linked up into national networks? And what about the new "on-line" media, such as the Internet, which interconnects thousands of diverse interest groups in a global electronic network?

The relationships between business and these multiple media are complex and often difficult to identify. As far as the mass media are concerned, they certainly represent the voice of the corporate establishment, which owns them and uses them skillfully to promote its worldview and values, focused on ever increasing material consumption – a value system that is profoundly anti-ecological. According to a widely accepted if cynical view, the primary function of contemporary mass media is to "deliver minds to advertisers – everything else is details." How, then, can we expect those media to influence business in any substantial way?

These questions seemed almost intractable to us. But if we were uncertain about what the conclusions of this chapter would be, we were quite sure about whom to ask to write it. As founder and editor-in-chief of the Minneapolis-based Utne Reader, *a "bimonthly digest of the best of the alternative media," Eric Utne is uniquely positioned to survey the whole contemporary media scene.*

Launched in 1984 with a circulation of 25,000, the magazine quickly became an unqualified success. Ten years later, its circulation had grown to over 300,000 and is recognized by publishing and advertising leaders as one of America's most influential and popular magazines. Prior to launching Utne Reader, *Utne served as director of New Ventures for the Wilson Learning Corporation, which offers seminars for executives. We could not think of anyone more qualified to disentangle the perplexing relationships between business and the media.*

As it turned out, Utne provided us with insights and conclusions we did not expect at all. After a brief but very instructive historical review at the beginning of the chapter, he focuses on the relationships between the media and community, and shows that one of the most harmful "second-order" effects of contemporary media has been to destroy local communities.

The same could be said of much contemporary business, which has accepted without question the concept of economy of scale. In search of ever lower marginal cost prices, production units have been pushed to ever bigger scales, and the sheer size of these huge manufacturing plants has disconnected business from the community. Jobs are no longer created where people live, so that people have to leave their community to commute to where the jobs are. Large, noisy, and polluting production units had to leave the inner cities, leaving broken communities in declining town centers behind.

Utne specifically includes electronic networks like the Internet in his critique of the media, discussing in some detail why "virtual communities" are not true communities and, contrary to widespread hopes, do not further democracy. His surprising conclusion is that one of the most important roles for today's media is to help create true communities, and that, rather than the media steering business, those communities will then by their very nature influence business in the direction of sustainability. This thesis is supported by the reader salons initiated by the Utne Reader *in 1992, which have blossomed into a nation-wide movement, involving nearly 20,000 participants in community building through face-to-face meetings and discussions of contemporary issues "from the heart."*

Utne reports that several print and electronic media have begun to join these efforts of community building, and he is convinced that playing an active role in community building will prove one of the most effective and most rewarding activities of business on the path toward sustainability.

Several years ago, we ran an article by Walter Carp in the *Utne Reader,* titled "Who decides what is news?" The author showed with a lot of examples that news stories in the United States are not researched but derived almost exclusively from official sources. The press seldom investigates. The news is funnelled through Capitol Hill. Objectivity is confused with passivity. Reporters are explicitly forbidden to comment, and the instrument for keeping them in line is manipulating access. There are threats to reporters and to publishers that if they don't toe the party line, their access to the country's political leaders will be reduced. In addition, of course, there's the influence of corporations through advertising. So business influences the media directly through its advertising money, and indirectly through the campaign funds to politicians. The question, then, is, what actual influence can the media have on business if they are victim to those influences?

I agree with Carp, but I'd like to approach the issue from a slightly different angle. It is indisputable that a major role of the media, acknowledged by some of their more honest representatives, is to deliver customers to business. There may not be nefarious motives in that; it's a consequence of the market economy. However, I want to make the point that for their long-term survival, business and media both have to reconceive their roles. Various media need to see their audience not just as consumers or markets, but as constituents. If they hope not only to survive but to carve out a vital and sustainable role for themselves, they must re-create themselves as convenors of community.

The sustainability of a community, and by extension that of the businesses in it, is inextricably bound to the community's overall health and vitality. Right now, the interests of the media and of business are very short-sighted, based as they are on concentrating power, ownership, and the messages communicated in very few people's hands. Their goals of economic growth, efficiency, and expansion put them in direct conflict with ecological balance and sustainability, which are mandatory for the health of all human and non-human communities.

The desire for stronger, cleaner, more cohesive communities is one of the principal concerns of people these days. They're yearning for a sense of connection and meaning in their lives. Unless the mass media begin to serve the interests of communities (where the vast majority of us live), rather than the interests of a few private individuals and corporations, people will eventually reject them – as they are now doing by creating their own community access television programs, desk-top publications, on-line computer conferences, and the like.

At various times in the history of magazines, to take just one medium as an example, precedents were set for journalists to promote the values and visions of sustainable culture. For their first 150 years, magazines were generally without advertising and often played quite an activist role in society. Only in the middle of the last century did advertising, through new forms of printing and especially the reproduction of photographs, turn magazines into vehicles for mass marketing. The wedding of ideas with commerce was a cultural innovation that had a sort of juggernaut effect. Very rapidly, magazines suddenly became much cheaper and therefore available to a much larger segment of the populace.

There was a reaction to this toward the end of the nineteenth century. Magazines and newspapers began to pay attention to the plight of the downtrodden and the underclass, and their provocative, no-holds-barred style became known as "muckraking." The media, as they were thought of then, thus had quite an active role as the "Fourth Estate," the provocateur that provided a counter-balance to the corruption of the entrenched powers-that-be.

During this century, the media's commitment to social justice has all but disappeared. The press has mostly become a mouthpiece for prevailing corporate and political values. There are exceptions: the underground press of the sixties, which was identified with "sex, drugs, and rock 'n roll," evolved into the alternative press of the seventies and spawned a tremendous number of progressive, outspoken publications. They represent the small voices on the edges of the mainstream that question the status quo. In terms of what the print media have to offer, these publications are the principal places for the expression of cutting-edge ideas and new values.

Putting out messages in a passionate, openly biased and quirky way is typical of the alternative press. In England and perhaps elsewhere in Europe, newspapers don't pretend to be as objective as do the *New York Times* and other American papers that consider themselves the journals of record. That's certainly true of the alternative press in this country as well; the kind of thinking that we like to see is advocacy thinking. Like the producers of network television, those of us working on alternative publications create the messages that we send out. Unlike the mainstream or corporate media, however, we don't pretend to be objective. Our writers put their progressive biases right in print.

What we're seeing now is that, although there are still many vehicles for spreading unconventional views, they are being overtaken in terms of readership and numbers by a proliferation of special-interest publications. These publications target self-selected groups of people who share common belief systems, lifestyles, interests and world views – what the *Yankelovich Monitor* calls "media communes." People segment themselves into special interest groups. They circle the wagons around a particular set of cultural norms and tend to be out of touch with anyone who has a different way of looking at things. There's not a true civic culture, a shared conception of the common good.

Businesses encourage these divisions through their promotion of specialized products and publications; the more "niche markets" there are, the more there is to make money on. We see huge chunks of our print publications and vast amounts of time on radio and television given over to corporate advertising. Computer on-line services are increasingly being used to relay commercial messages as well. More and more of people's time is spent gazing into computer, television, and video screens or sticking their nose into tabloids and news-magazines that feed the mind but not the soul.

The consequences of this shift are only now becoming apparent. There are first-order consequences and second-order consequences of technology. For example, the first-order consequence of the invention of the internal combustion engine was a shift in people's mode of transportation from the horse to the horseless carriage, the automobile. A second-order consequence was the creation of the suburbs. We totally rearranged our living patterns. What is the second-order consequence of the media? As we've gone from print to radio, then to television, and now to on-line and multimedia communications, the first-order consequence is that people would shift from one medium to another. But the second order consequence is that our lives and our belief systems have become increasingly mediated.

What the media have really done is destroyed community, and that has a profound impact. Whether it's the corporate media, or well-meaning, non-advertising, non-commercial media – the effect of the medium itself, of whichever kind it may be, is to distance people from their genuine, flesh-and-blood community and link them to anonymous others who share their interests. It's really a kind of identity politics.

So we have these media communes, or what many people are calling "networks." There's a terrible danger of confusing networking – whether on-line or not – with the real joy of true community. The Internet is not a real community; it is simply people who are involved in networks. The difference is that in networks people arrange themselves according to common interests, and by choice. You can choose to be in or you can opt out. In true communities, diverse people are required to deal with each other, to "mix it up" face to face and to work through their differences. Living in community is not easy, but can be tremendously rewarding. It teaches us tolerance. That's the basic ingredient of democracy: finding a way to get along with each other. Rather than separating ourselves from people with whom we disagree, moving them out of our circle, we must learn how to deal with them.

Most of the people on this planet live in real communities, but most North American college-educated people tend to arrange themselves in networks. They work with, they live with, and they hang out with people like themselves, with similar educational levels. They've come to mistrust people who are differently educated. They don't know them; they're distant from them. There is not a democratic foundation to their lives.

Jeffersonian democracy was based on the belief that the greatest wisdom lies in the majority of the people, not in the few "best and brightest" who would plan for the rest of us. That's a very different model of government than the one we have now. Christopher Lasch wrote in our Salon issue four years ago that what is necessary for true democracy is an educated, informed citizenry, but that information and education are not necessarily academic. What we have now is an enormous amount of information that washes over people, and that is taken in passively if it is taken in at all. The mass media continue to act as the corporate voice, but the public is not listening anymore. People are simply losing the capacity to listen. The sea of information everyone is swimming in is completely cluttered and congested. Everyone is competing for attention, trying to break through the clutter, and people quite naturally, I think, as a survival mechanism, tune it out.

That, of course, is not democracy. Democracy is an activity, a process. It is based on people's experiences, relationships, and common learning. The only way to have a truly informed citizenry, an active and motivated citizenry, is through live, personal discussion and debate. The information we need – in fact, more than the information, the knowledge and the wisdom – comes by word of mouth. Think of what life was like before the advent of commercial media. People got their news from each other, through story-telling and small talk, through shared observations. You'd learn about when to plant, and what the weather meant, and what was happening in the community. But increasingly the media have been telling us about people we don't know, who are at a distance from us, and convincing us that what's going on elsewhere is more important than what's going on right here.

As the media have evolved, they have separated communities. But now, they *can* become a connective tissue. They can facilitate the shift from a market-oriented culture to a community-oriented culture. They can promote genuine democracy and connectedness by focusing on that which is really relevant to the lives of everyday people.

How? Not so much by exerting pressure on business directly as by introducing its readers and viewers to each other. Most media represent a one-way broadcast model, with the information coming from the center and radiating out to the periphery. Editors and station managers often feel happy and successful if they get some feedback to the center in the form of audience response. But what they're not doing is introducing those people around them, their constituents, to each other. That's where community happens.

Utne Reader had a conference some time ago on "Media and the Environment," which explored the advocacy role of the media with regard to environmental problems. At this conference, we brought some of our subscribers together. When we introduced them to each other and invited them to speak from the heart about the things they cared about and believed in, genuine new relationships were formed.

This made me realize that we should try to do this not for just these few dozen or few hundred people at this conference, but for all our subscribers who would like to meet. So we ran a little ad in the Salon issue that invited our subscribers to let us know if they'd like to meet other *Utne Reader* subscribers in their area. In other words, we introduced our readers to each other. Nearly 10,000 people responded, and now over 20,000 people are meeting monthly in each other's living rooms to talk about the things they care about, and often to do other things. Some are getting married; others are starting businesses or schools or co-housing projects. All kinds of things have come out of it. And our salons are just a little tip of the iceberg of an enormous craving people have for human interaction and true community.

As a result of what we did, the *Minneapolis Tribune* started community roundtable discussions that they've been promoting in the newspaper for the last two years. As of September 1994, 171 newspapers around the country have gotten involved in similar efforts in what has come to be known as "public journalism." Not only is it a service to the community, it's in the business interest of newspapers to do this kind of thing. People who are connected to their communities read their local newspapers, so a natural goal of newspapers should be to hook people into their communities. When people are brought together and given an excuse to speak about what's most important to them, collaborations and connections are made, and community begins.

The *Wichita Eagle*, in Kansas, is also part of this "public journalism" movement. Starting in 1990, the paper began to vigorously hold political candidates accountable for their positions. They repeatedly ran a feature that outlined candidates' stands on key political issues and news stories that covered these controversial issues in depth. They analyzed the candidates' publicity for accuracy, published a sizable "Voter's Guide" just before Election Day, and sponsored TV public service announcements that encouraged citizens to vote. Research showed that voter turnout was way up as a result, and that people's understanding of the issues also increased substantially. This experiment led to the Wichita Peoples Project, in which the newspaper collaborated with a TV and radio station to invite citizens "to share ideas about how to regain control over the systems that control our lives" and to explore the "core values" of the community.

Another constructive use of the media is a televised public forum in El Paso, Texas, called "Paso del Norte." Several times a year, with the help of the National Issues Forum, citizen discussion groups come together to grapple with a specific community problem. Information that outlines a variety of viewpoints on the issue is made available at the local library. The group discussions are moderated by trained facilitators, and a relevant film clip on the subject is often shown.

Each discussion group then sends representatives to a televised, prime-time, call-in forum. On the Sunday before the forum, the local newspaper carries an article on the upcoming television show topic, along with a "ballot" that solicits citizen opinion. The opinions of every caller to the forum and every participant in the discussion groups are tabulated along with the ballots sent to the newspaper, and then sent to policy makers. It's a clear example of how the media can usefully promote citizen discussion and debate.

In *The Quickening of America: Rebuilding Our Nation, Remaking Our Lives*, by Paul DuBois and Frances Moore Lappé, a number of innovations are suggested which, if adopted by media outlets, would make them much more responsive to their communities:[1]

- Conducting surveys or town meetings to learn citizens' concerns;
- publishing in-depth articles connecting social issues to people's everyday lives;
- pressing candidates aggressively for clear, full explanations of positions;
- publishing special voter guides;
- repeating issue summaries and analyses several times during electoral campaigns;
- sponsoring public-service TV spots to encourage voting;
- connecting people to citizens' groups working on particular issues;
- furnishing a meeting place for citizens to discuss key issues;
- forming task forces to sponsor discussions of key issues;
- transforming the "letters to the editor" section into a real dialogue, organized by key topics;
- starting an expanded community bulletin board that provides information about events;
- launching a "citizen of the week" profile highlighting community problem-solvers;
- initiating a regular column written by students and/or teachers about reforms needed or under way in the local schools.

As Lappé and DuBois point out, "As long as the media are a mere commodity, responsibility for their use rests with the shareholders of media conglomerates. The shareholders' goal, understandably, is the highest return on their investment. But as the media become communication tools in a living democracy, they no longer are simply a commodity. They also become a *community good*."

Now, *Utne Reader* discussion groups are a kind of media communes in their own right. Our readers are a very unusual, highly educated, and involved group, and we're bringing them together with like-minded people. In a sense, they begin as self-selected networks

---

[1] Frances Moore Lappé and Paul Martin DuBois, *The Quickening of America*, Jossey-Bass, San Francisco, 1994.

of the kind I'm criticizing. But when these people get together and they create a level of intimacy, they start looking for people who are different from them to bring into the conversation. We think the next stage of our salon movement is to work with other organizations of very different political, social, and cultural points of view, and to have a much larger conversation.

This fits very nicely with what Sheldon Hackney at the National Endowment for the Humanities is encouraging. The central project under his tenure as the head of the NEH will be to create what he calls a National Conversation among Americans all over the country. In town meetings, church basements, and people's living rooms, they will talk about what it means to be an American. Hackney feels discussion groups are the way to really get things going.

If people start reasserting community and reconnecting to community, this will change the nature of their relationship to business. They will be stakeholders rather than mere consumers. As a result, those who are offering products will have to become more responsive to their dictates. Business will recognize that for its own sustainability, it must help people become active seekers of information through discussion and debate with their fellow citizens.

To summarize, I have sort of side-stepped the question of how media can steer business toward sustainability. In my view, the emerging new role of media is to help create community, and a true community by its very nature will influence business in the direction of sustainability. In other words, the influence will go from media to community and from community to business. Then, of course, I would also suggest to business that it has a role in helping create community, and that such a role will make business more viable. People may be suspicious of that role at first, just as they are suspicious of "greenwashing." But advocacy-oriented entrepreneurs have found again and again that they will enlist people's allegiance if what they do is sincere and effective.

Part Two:
Incentives

7

The Role of Government

Monika Griefahn

We begin this section on incentives for business to move toward sustainability with a chapter on the role of government, and to do so we have chosen Germany as an example of a country in which governments, both at the national and state (Land) levels, play significant roles in environmental affairs. In fact, their roles must be seen as outright activist by the standards of most industrialized countries, and German governmental measures to promote sustainability are far in advance of those elsewhere.

This strong environmental role of government in Germany is a consequence of a long and successful tradition of environmental activism. Since the mid-seventies the so-called "alternative scene," which strongly embraces ecological values, has become an integral part of German cultural life; and since the early eighties Green politics has been a stable feature of the political landscape. Although the number of Green voters in local, regional, and national elections rarely exceeds 10 percent, the popular support of the Green agenda is much higher, and the "Greens," as they are commonly called, have succeeded in strongly influencing the nature of the political dialogue.

From the beginning, one of the most ingenious strategies of the Green movement has been to operate both inside and outside the political structures – inside as parliamentarians and government representatives, and outside as part of the global network of NGOs. Monika Griefahn personifies this strategy in a unique way. A former leading Greenpeace activist and founding member of the Green Party, she subsequently joined the Social Democratic Party and became Minister of the Environment in the state of Lower Saxony (Niedersachsen), the state that will host the World Expo dedicated to technology and the environment in the year 2000. Griefahn is a politician with a strong ecological vision who remains loyal to her ideals and has managed to implement many of them within the local government, industry, science, and society at large.

From her unique vantage point as an activist turned government official, Griefahn explains in this chapter the approaches taken and under consideration in her area, which include: advanced research on product redesign; reorientation of energy policy; and forums bringing together problem-solving groups drawn from management, labor, science, the environmental movement, and the political world. The vision emerging in Germany is of modernized, highly advanced industries linked in closed-cycle relationships, moving toward renewable energy sources and greater conservation.

Twenty-five years of environmental politics in Germany have yielded sobering results: the destruction of the environment continues and has already reached dramatic proportions. Undesirable developments in economy and society have piled up our ecological debts to such an extent that even our health is increasingly affected. This has involved children, in particular, for quite some time, for whom allergies, asthma, and neurodermatitis are no longer exceptions.

What is also appalling is the damage to the environment: two-thirds of the German forests have been damaged so far. Our land development is as high as ever so that even the last few natural habitats in Germany are in serious jeopardy with the consequence that more and more domestic species of flora and fauna are dying out. In addition, numerous pollutants poison our air, our water, our soils, and our food every day, at the same time increasing the hazards to the environment on a global scale by boosting the greenhouse effect and thinning out the vital ozone layer. Although this is a description of conditions in Germany, it is highly likely that the situation is similar in most of the other industrialized countries.

Anybody who – like many people in business – demands a moratorium in the field of environmental politics or even a weakening of environmental standards shows a lack of responsibility. Rather than a standstill in or withdrawal from environmental politics we need an extensive ecological reorganization of the economy and society. In order to initiate or promote this modernization process, environmental politics must be accorded priority as an across-the-board task, i.e., environmental politicians have to take interdepartmental action. It must be our aim that the decisions taken in all political fields from economic through transportation to foreign policies must be reviewed for their ecological impact.

Modern environmental policy, as I see it, must no longer restrict itself to removing waste or to reducing the pollution of water, soil and air by means of filters or catalytic converters – for these pollutants will only reappear elsewhere. Environmental politics must be preventive politics and aim at developing and enforcing products and production procedures incorporating the idea of environmental soundness "from the cradle to the grave." This will help to avoid the generation of many pollutants from the very beginning, and any residues will be recycled in an environmentally friendly way.

In 1984, former German chancellor Willy Brandt outlined the priorities of the ecological modernization concept, which is to take up three interrelated challenges: unemployment, threats to the environment, and technological change. The solution he offered was that we must create a framework in which environmentally useful and sophisticated production procedures and products are developed. That would help the environment and at the same time create secure jobs with a promising future. What is necessary, according to Brandt, is a profound economic reform resulting in an industrialized society using raw materials and energy economically and efficiently. Such an ecologically oriented modern economic policy will strengthen the prospects of the economy.

Today, these statements are more topical than ever. Ecology must not be defined as an add-on to economics, but must be recognized as the basis of any responsible economic activity. Business activities must be guided by what is ecologically required. In the medium term only goods should be manufactured and used which are in line with the principle of natural ecological cycles.

Thus the ecological reorganization of our economy extends from the product concept through the manufacturing process to consumption and recycling and the completion of substance-related cycles. It requires an ecological assessment of the substances, compounds, and processes used and includes all forms of energy production and energy conversion.

A suitable way of enforcing such production and consumption principles is the use of the instruments of the market economy. The levying of taxes or specific fees on certain environmentally harmful manufacturing processes, products or services can often bring about their replacement by environmentally friendly alternatives faster than sole application of administrative regulations. In Lower Saxony, the introduction of two environmental taxes has already achieved considerable controlling effects within a short period.

The waste tax levied by the state of Lower Saxony is based on the principle that those who protect the environment will be rewarded while those who pollute or consume it have to pay. According to the law governing waste taxes, it is intended as a control designed to promote waste avoidance and utilization of residual materials by trade and industry. The tax has to be paid by the generators of waste requiring special supervision and by the operators of waste disposal facilities importing such waste to Lower Saxony. The tax rate is coupled to hazardousness, avoidability, and recyclability of the waste. The revenue from the tax will also be used to fund avoidance and recycling technologies as well as the clean-up of polluted areas.

A similar objective is pursued with the water withdrawal tax. Its aim is to promote water-saving efforts and the installation of closed water cycles. The tax rate is coupled to the purpose and origin of the water withdrawn or discharged. This tax is intended to finance not only the compensatory payments for restricted use of farmland in water reserve areas, but also water and nature protection measures, a river banks renaturalization program, information on water protection, and a water-saving program.

However, it should be emphasized that the German constitution does not give the state governments much leeway in promoting ecological behavior by applying economic instruments. Therefore, the possibilities available to the state governments need to be complemented on a national level by an ecological tax reform making labor less expensive by cutting incidental wage costs while making the consumption of the environment more expensive by means of higher taxes on energy and raw materials. Within the scope of an ecological reorganization, the following major objectives have to be achieved:

1. Development and introduction of new ecological products and processes
2. Ecological reorientation of trade and industry
3. Profound reorientation of the energy policy from nuclear to solar energy

Development of New and Future-Capable Product

For the ecological modernization of the economy we need future-capable and long-life products which require a minimum of material and energy to be manufactured, which contribute to waste avoidance, and which do not leave behind any pollutants. In this context it is the task of politics to create a climate favorable to innovation by pursuing economic, research, and environmental policies which are strictly in line with ecological requirements. So far there has been a lack of investments in environmentally friendly and innovative products which are suited to secure industrial production. The government must create a framework in which companies that adapt their production or services to ecological requirements can swiftly launch their products and achieve economic success.

Unlike Germany, Japan has long since recognized the importance of such an ecologization of the economy. It is essential to capitalize on the Japanese experience: the Japanese Ministry for International Trade and Industry (MITI) and industry itself founded – in 1990 – the Research Institute for Innovative Technology on the Earth (RITE). This institute is concerned mainly with the development of products and production methods that contribute to climate protection. Their projects include research in the fields of carbon dioxide absorption, new cooling agents, or compostable plastics. For certain projects, RITE cooperates also with private enterprises and other institutions. One notable feature of this institute is the close cooperation between the government and industry in the joint development of environmentally friendly production processes and substitute substances. In Germany, on the other hand, companies often do this only under the pressure of law and then in fierce competition among each other. The result is that in Germany about seven companies are developing the same number of CFC substitutes whereas the Japanese are jointly working on the development of a single substance. This, of course, saves money and time – time which is used for the launching of advanced ecological products.

Another example is fuel-efficient cars. The Japanese have announced plans to introduce an 80-mpg car within three years. Efforts are also being made in this field in the United States. Together with General Motors, the energy expert Amory Lovins has been developing a new car within the scope of the "Super Cars" project for several years. According to Lovins, a quantum leap might be possible in this field. An efficiency of 394–448 mpg for a four-person car and a 100- to 1000-fold reduction of emissions could be achieved by an appropriate design of the body, by a marked reduction of weight and air resistance, by a marked reduction of transmission losses in the engine, and by a new hybrid electric drive. Lovins thinks that this might result in a realistic improvement of the overall efficiency by a factor of five to fifteen. Mass production could start in the year 2000.

For a future-capable industry this can only mean expediting corresponding projects and launching the resultant products. There are two important measures that might help facilitate such innovations:

1. Founding research and development institutes for promising products such as degradable and environmentally friendly plastics;
2. Establishing standing fora where companies, labor unions, scientists, politicians, and citizens jointly work out the general conditions for innovations.

In Lower Saxony, we have now gained some experience with such a forum in which representatives from management and labor, on the one hand, and from science, environmental associations, and politics on the other discuss the general conditions for the reorganization of production. The subjects dealt with are the reappropriation of research funds, type and objective of tax incentives, quality control, and ecological balance sheets, as well as problems of public relations and marketing. The first forum involved the plastics-processing industry. After an experts' meeting, a round table of company representatives, scientists, and representatives from labor unions and environmental associations continued the talks, discussing in particular all the problems with regard to plastics – from production through utilization to disposal. All parties involved are aware of the fact that forward-looking strategies must be developed not only for solving ecological problems but also for securing the future of the chemical industry in Germany. Even today, mass-produced plastics like PVC are manufactured at lower costs in the former Eastern Bloc countries or in Saudi Arabia than in Germany. DM 1.20 must be spent to produce one kilogram in Germany whereas the same quantity costs only DM 0.80 in Asia. The consequence is that such products will be imported in the future so that soon nobody will be able to make money or provide jobs with them in Germany. However, we are determined to and will prevent the chemical industry from slipping into the same kind of crisis as the steel industry. Another aspect is the high energy costs for plastics. Here, too, we are at a crossroads: Which plastics will we need in future? Cheap products with high disposal costs or high-quality special products and biologically degradable plastics which may be more expensive to produce but easy to recycle or dispose of?

The answer is obvious: What we need is an innovative boost in the development and launching of environmentally friendly and internationally competitive products and services. To achieve this, close cooperation among government, industry, science, and society will be indispensable.

Closed-Cycle Economy and Ecological Enterprises

For this reorganization industry requires incentives – in terms of both money and concepts. A forward-looking concept is the realization of a closed-cycle economy which – from the biological as well as the technological point of view – can take back almost anything it has produced and put it into the production cycle again, the consumer being the only interim user. Most consumer goods fit into one of three categories: non-durable goods, durable goods, or goods which finally end up as waste. The last must be the smallest quantity in the future. Non-durable goods that are used up completely or are subject to wear and tear in the course of time such as shampoo, detergents, shoes, or tires must be fully biologically degradable. Durable goods are not purchased for their own sake but for the specific service they offer: cars, razors, TV sets, or computers. In the future they will have to be designed in such a way that they can be fully disassembled. Above all they will have to be taken back directly by the manufacturer. This will be the only way to ensure that the manufacturers change over to environmentally friendly production methods.

At present, those durable goods stand for a gigantic waste of raw materials. A TV set contains more than 4,000 different chemicals – resources as well as pollutants. The production of a TV picture tube alone requires as much energy as the production of all glass vessels the average consumer hauls to the public glass collection bins in the course of his/her life. In the future this material must be reused by the manufacturer, who must also be responsible for disassembly.

If this kind of product responsibility becomes general practice, the next step will only be logical: the manufacturer will remain the owner of his/her product from the outset. Durable goods such as TV sets or computers will then not be purchased any more, but leased. For the consumer wants to take advantage of the utility value only, not of the material value. He or she wants to watch TV. Today, however, when buying a TV set consumers automatically become the owners of plastics, cathode ray tube, and manganese, i.e., expensive reusable material or hazardous wastes that are of no use at all to them.

What is therefore urgently required is improved environmental liability as well as extended product liability and responsibility. In addition, tools like eco-leasing need to be developed and put to use.

In the ecological modernization of the economy a key role is played by waste policy. For instance, multiple-use systems can and must be promoted more intensively in many fields. What is basically required is a closed-cycle economy law which really deserves this name because it not only controls the flow of waste but also requires substances and products to meet certain standards. The compromise negotiated by the German Bundesrat and Bundestag[1] with regard to the Closed-Cycle Economy Act proposed by the former minister for the environment, Klaus Toepfer, constitutes merely an improved waste disposal act. Improvements could be achieved only through the initiative of those federal states governed by the SPD. For example, waste avoidance is accorded absolute priority. What remains to be done now is to further develop waste management into ecological substance management governed by the principle of sustainable development and aiming at a reduction in the quantity of substances, a multiple and efficient use of substances, the deceleration of the flow of substances, and the closure of substance cycles. This can really help to avoid waste and establish utilization cycles. Ecological substance management is made possible via the product responsibility of the manufacturers. In developing and realizing an ecological substance policy, we will utilize the findings of the German Bundestag commission of inquiry into the "Protection of Man and Environment," which has furnished many ideas and suggestions.

What is important for the ecological modernization of the economy is, of course, the ecological orientation of the enterprises themselves. In this context, there are many positive approaches which must be improved, promoted and broadened. In the last few years "ecological pioneers" from trade and industry have founded organizations such as the "Bundesdeutscher Arbeitskreis für umweltbewußtes Management – B.A.U.M."[2] or "Future." Together with those organizations we intend to further develop and apply instruments for the ecological

---

[1] Upper and lower houses of the German parliament
[2] Federal Association for Environmentally Conscious Management, the acronym B.A.U.M. meaning "tree"

orientation of company policies such as the ecological audit regulation of the European Union or environmental controlling. In Lower Saxony a research project investigated the environmental management information system. Among other things, this study revealed that environmental controlling not only highlights widely known environmental problems in the companies, but also offers approaches for cutting costs and increasing production. The introduction of such systems in individual enterprises, especially in small trade firms, must be promoted.

In this context it would be useful to further develop – together with science and the appropriate associations – other instruments for ecological modernization such as ecological balance sheets for individual products or product line analyses. While ecological balance sheets provide an analysis of the entire life cycle of a product and its ecological impact, assessing the resultant substance and energy requirements as well as the resultant environmental pollution, product line analyses also cover the socio-economic effects. They register, analyze, and assess the benefits of the products concerned.

From Nuclear to Solar Industry

Since Chernobyl, nobody seriously doubts that relying on nuclear energy means following the wrong track. This allegedly clean and safe way of generating electrical power has presented us with dilapidated reactors in Eastern Europe, a still-unsolved final disposal problem with huge amounts of radioactive waste, dangerous transports of plutonium around half the globe, and a flourishing black market in radioactive substances that has assumed alarming proportions. The further use of nuclear energy would be irresponsible, as new disasters cannot be ruled out. Nuclear technology is a dinosaur technology which, with its large-scale power plants, does not support energy-saving efforts and which, because of its capital intensity, ties up major financial resources required for a rational environmentally friendly energy system. Funds and research capacities employed so far for nuclear energy can and must be put to better use elsewhere: future energy supply must be based on regenerative energies such as wind, sun, and biomass. This is where the course must be set in the next few years. Therefore the Lower Saxony government intends to pull out of the use of nuclear energy and calls upon the federal government to substitute a Nuclear Energy Replacement Act for the

Nuclear Energy Act. A corresponding Bundesrat initiative rejects the construction of new nuclear power plants.

What is necessary instead is to begin using renewable energies, in particular solar energy. So far, renewable sources of energy have met only a minor part of our energy requirements, but as in many other countries this can be traced back to the fact that they were paid little attention under research and technology policies that prevailed in Germany during the last few decades. Nevertheless, renewable energy sources have been booming in Germany for some time:

- The electric capacity generated by wind energy has doubled within one year. In 1993 alone, 600 new wind power machines were built. Lower Saxony is trying to optimize the economic utilization of wind energy by promoting projects such as the 1,000-megawatt wind power program. This has resulted not only in new environmentally sound energy sources, but also in new jobs. (For example, in a Lower Saxony company that had as few as 20 employees in 1985, the number of personnel rose to approximately 400 in less than ten years due to the boom in demand for wind-power plants.)
- Associations in the solar energy trade and industry are registering a steady rise of 25 percent per year in the number of orders for solar energy systems, with corresponding profits achieved not only by the manufacturers but also by the sellers and craftspeople who increasingly extend their business activities to the field of solar energy technology. Unlike Germany where the so-called 1,000-roof project introduced in 1991 has long since expired, Japan can serve as an example in this field. The Japanese government recently decided on a 70,000-roof program, paving the way for a new solar energy industry that creates new jobs, particularly in medium-sized businesses.
- Therefore, the German Social Democratic Party has suggested that the German federal government should introduce a 100,000-roof program to promote solar energy technology. The production of solar energy systems will become an important branch of industry and an element of competition in the world market. Within the next 20 years, hundreds of thousands of new jobs can be created through the production of solar cells, solar collectors, and wind-power plants. Buildings equipped with solar energy systems will also offer excellent opportunities for workshops and medium-sized businesses. The same applies to the utilization of wind energy. The funding of such forward-looking promotion and launching programs would be ensured by part of the revenue from an ecological tax reform.

- In addition, measures must be devised that promote the rational use and conservation of energy. Energy consumption continues to rise on a global scale. Germany ranks fifth among the energy consumers worldwide and first among the European Union countries, where our per capita energy consumption exceeds the average by twenty-two per cent. Much could be achieved politically in the field of energy by changing the general conditions: an investment program designed to promote the rational use of energy and renewable energy sources could counteract this development and foster the construction of combined heat and power plants and the launching of renewable energy sources. In addition, the law governing the feed-in of electric power from renewable energy sources needs to be improved and administrative obstacles blocking the use of renewable energy must be eliminated. Changing the appropriate building laws could promote both passive and active use of energy, with public buildings and federally financed low-cost housing being important sectors. Finally, renewable energy sources would have to be given priority in research and development policies. Of course, this applies also to the EU as a whole; the focus of research must be shifted from fusion research to renewable energy sources and a corresponding program launched for the European market.

In Lower Saxony, ecological reorientation of business is being promoted by a number of concrete measures. One instrument is the so-called "ecological fund for economic development." To realize its environmental objectives the Lower Saxon government has complemented its fund for economic development with an ecological aspect, extending economic development beyond growth and job considerations to promote environmental protection measures for the ecological reorientation and modernization of production processes. Promotion takes place in close coordination between the Lower Saxon Ministry for Economy, Technology and Transport and the Lower Saxon Ministry for the Environment in order to do justice to the interconnection of the portfolios of Environment and Economy.

Under a binding procurement guideline, all authorities administering public funds in Lower Saxony must ensure that any equipment or material procured meets the criteria of environmental compatibility. When placing contracts the authorities, who in total play a significant role on the demand side, must contribute in an exemplary way towards reaching the aims of avoiding waste, minimizing pollutants in the waste, recycling substances, and saving energy and water. In the field of federally financed low-cost housing, buildings which

105

meet high standards of energy conservation are eligible for special government grants.

In order to reduce environmentally harmful motorized individual traffic the Lower Saxony government has offered all employees cheap tickets for buses and trains, thus setting an example which has been copied by several companies and public authorities. Finally, an energy program and an energy institute provide instruments to promote energy conservation measures and regenerative energy sources. While the energy institute has the primary task of providing concrete support to enterprises, local authorities, housing companies, and utility companies by giving advice and developing pilot projects for the ecological reorganization of energy supply or utilization, the energy program is designed to promote the pull-out of nuclear energy use without a rise in carbon dioxide emissions.

Ecological Pioneering

An ecological modernization of the economy is also vital for global environmental protection to control the greenhouse effect and protect the ozone layer. It is in particular the OECD countries which must meet their international commitments and no longer delay in adopting national climate protection programs. As is well known, Germany has undertaken to reduce the carbon dioxide emissions by at least one quarter by the year 2005. However, this objective will only be achieved if the measures for the ecological modernization of economy and society are consistently geared towards reaching the overall aim of sustainable development. It was as long ago as 1987 that the UNCED Brundtland Report defined that aim roughly as follows: "Sustainable development means development which satisfies the needs of the present without running the risk that future generations are unable to satisfy their own needs."

To be able to preserve our natural basis of living we need sustainable development all over the world. The industrialized countries, in particular Germany, must pioneer in the ecological modernization of the economy. Because the way of life in the rich industrialized countries is a decisive factor for the chances of survival of humankind, we are determined to initiate a policy of sustainable development in our own country. Germany is one of the countries responsible for conserving the global natural environment and ensuring sustainable development in the countries of the South. The commitments made at the UNCED conference in Rio must be met. What is necessary is a better orientation of the international institutions towards this overall objective, including the convening of an international debt conference. An ecological modernization of our economy will also generate the know-how required for sustainable development all over the world. In his book *Earth in the Balance: Ecology and Human Spirit*, U.S. Vice-President Al Gore sets out the principle of the necessary course correction, which governs our activities as well: "We must make the rescue of the environment the central organizational principle for civilization."

8

Ecological Tax Reform

Herman E. Daly

The ecological pioneer companies mentioned throughout this book have managed to make big strides toward sustainability while at the same time being successful in terms of the bottom line. In our present economic system, such an integration of economics and ecology is not easy, because it is strongly discouraged by current tax policies.

In most industrial countries today, we tax what we should encourage – jobs and real income – and we reward what we should discourage – pollution and resource depletion. These tax policies give business strong signals to maximize energy use and waste, favor virgin materials over recycled ones, and seek quantitative rather than qualitative growth – all of these leading away from ecological sustainability and toward ultimate ecological and economic collapse. In addition, by taxing labor and income, governments reduce employment and help create social instability.

Herman Daly is a distinguished economist who has argued for several decades that it is possible to design a radically different economic system, one that incorporates the basic principles of ecology. Daly was Senior Economist in the Environment Department of the World Bank from 1988 to 1994 and is currently Senior Research Scholar at the School of Public Affairs of the University of Maryland. He is co-founder and associate editor of the journal Ecological Economics *(Elsevier), has authored over one hundred articles in professional journals and anthologies, and is the author of several widely acclaimed books, including his classic* Steady-State Economics *(1977; second edition 1991) and* For the Common Good: Redirecting the Economy

Toward Community, the Environment, and a Sustainable Future
(1994; co-authored with John Cobb).

*In this far-seeing chapter, Daly provides a careful analysis of an
ecological tax reform of the type that is now under study in several
European countries. He demonstrates that economic arguments can be
used not to reinforce the status quo, but to create a tax system that
would provide powerful incentives for business to move toward sustainability.*

Introduction: Tax Labor and Income Less, and Tax Resource Throughput More

In the past it has been considered desirable for governments to sub-
sidize resource throughput* to stimulate growth. Thus energy, water,
fertilizer, and even deforestation are still frequently subsidized. To its
credit the World Bank (1992) has generally opposed these subsidies,
but they remain widespread. It is necessary, however, to go beyond
removal of explicit financial subsidies to the removal of implicit environmental subsidies as well. By "implicit environmental subsidies"
I mean external costs to the community that are not charged to the
commodities whose production generates them.

Economists have long advocated internalizing external costs either
by calculating and charging Pigouvian taxes (after economist A. C.
Pigou, who advocated taxes which when added to marginal private
costs make the price equal to marginal social costs), or by Coasian
redefinition of property rights (after Ronald Coase, who advocated
property rights extensions such that values that used to be public
property, and thus not valued in markets, become private property
whose values are protected by their new owners). These solutions are
elegant in theory, but often quite difficult in practice. A blunter but
much more operational instrument would be simply to shift our tax
base away from labor and income onto throughput. We have to raise
public revenue somehow, and the present system is highly distor-

---

*The term "throughput" is an inelegant but highly useful derivative of the terms input and
output. The matter-energy that goes into a system and eventually comes out is what goes
through – the "throughput," as engineers have dubbed it. A biologist's synonym might be the
"metabolic flow" by which an organism maintains itself. This physical flow connects the economy to the environment at both ends, and is of course subject to the physical laws of conservation and entropy.

tionary: by taxing labor and income in the face of high unemployment in nearly all countries, we are discouraging exactly what we want more of. The present signal to firms is to shed labor and substitute more capital and resource throughput to the extent feasible. It would be better to economize on throughput because of the depletion and pollution associated with it, and at the same time to use more labor because of the high social benefits associated with reducing unemployment.

More fundamentally, as we have moved from an "empty" to a "full" world, the remaining natural capital has more and more come to play the role of limiting factor, a role previously played by man-made capital. Our economizing effort must always focus on the limiting factor, according to economic theory. The theory has stayed the same but the identity of the limiting factor has changed. To economize on natural capital we must raise its price relative to man-made capital. We must do this by policy, such as ecological tax reform. There are many reasons why the market will not automatically bring about the needed increase in price on natural capital:

- Natural capital, for example, is the stock of trees in a forest that yields a flow of cut timber, or the population of fish in the sea that yields a flow of caught fish. The annual flow of cut timber and caught fish would be "natural income." Natural capital also provides a flow of natural services such as CO_2 absorption, nutrient recycling, regulation of temperature, rainfall runoff, etc. Natural capital is common property, and lack of private ownership means it is unpriced.
- On the source side the running down of natural capital stocks and inventories increases short-run supply and lowers price. If all ranchers decided to liquidate their herds over the next five years and go out of business (in order, say, to invest in chickens), we would not be surprised to see falling beef prices for five years. That will not hold, however, in the sixth year.
- There are possibilities for substitution of abundant resources for scarce ones, within limits not yet reached.
- Externalizing costs of extraction and production keeps resource prices lower than they otherwise would and should be.
- Demand as well as supply affects price, of course, and ruling the demands of many interested parties out of the market keeps prices lower. For example, future generations do not bid in today's markets, and even the present's provision for the future is cut short by the practice of discounting. The survival needs of nonhuman

species, like those of future humans, are not expressed in markets.

- Investment by the North in technologies to speedily extract resources in the South results in lower resources prices and a transfer of value from South to North.
- As will be discussed more in the next section, market prices only solve the problem of efficient allocation – and do so only by taking prior solutions to the problems of just distribution and sustainable scale as given. To count on market prices to solve the scale problem is a "category mistake," like trying to drive a screw with a hammer.

There is a growing consensus among a broad range of stakeholders in the U.S., and even more so in Europe, concerning the need to reform tax systems to tax "bads" rather than "goods." Taxes have substantive incentive effects which need to be considered and utilized more effectively. The most comprehensive proposed implementation of this idea is coming to be known under the general heading of "ecological tax reform" (von Weizsäcker and Jesinghaus 1992, Costanza and Daly 1992, Passell 1992, Repetto et al. 1992, Hawken 1993, Costanza 1994). Earlier discussions of similar schemes were given by Page (1977) who considered a national severance tax, and Daly (1977) who discussed a depletion quota auction which is roughly equivalent.

Shifting the tax base to throughput induces greater throughput efficiency, and internalizes in a gross, blunt manner the externalities from depletion and pollution. True, the exact external costs will not have been precisely calculated and attributed to exactly those activities that caused them, as could theoretically be accomplished with a Pigouvian tax that aims to equate marginal social costs and benefits for each activity. But those calculations and attributions are so difficult and uncertain that insisting on them would be equivalent to a full-employment act for econometricians and bureaucrats, and prolonged unemployment and environmental degradation for everyone else.

Politically the shift toward ecological taxes could be sold under the banner of revenue neutrality. However, the income tax structure should be maintained so as to keep some progressivity in the overall tax structure by taxing very high incomes and subsidizing very low incomes. But the bulk of public revenue would be raised from taxes on throughput, which could be levied at the depletion or pollution end, or both. To minimize disruption, the shift could be carried out gradually by a pre-announced schedule. This shift should be a key part of structural adjustment, but should be pioneered in the North.

Indeed, sustainable development itself must be achieved in the North first. It is absurd to expect any sacrifice for sustainability in the South if similar measures have not first been taken in the North. Later we will return to the theme of a North/South bargain as the international context for national policies of ecological tax reform.

The basic goal of ecological tax reform is to limit the throughput of resources to an ecologically sustainable scale and composition relative to the ecosystem, a goal until recently neglected. But the more traditional goal of efficient allocation of resources is also served by this instrument because it raises the tax on bads and lowers the tax on goods – it internalizes externalities in a blunt general way, without getting stuck in the morass of calculating Pigouvian taxes and fretting over secondary general equilibrium consequences. Another economic goal, of distributive equity, is both helped and hindered. The throughput tax is basically a capturing for public purposes of the scarcity rent to natural capital as economic and demographic growth increases its value. Rent is defined as any payment above the minimum necessary supply price for a factor of production. For land the necessary supply price is zero (no one has to produce it), so all payment for land is rent. Some payment for resources is rent. Rent increases with demand for land. Since rent is an unearned surplus there are strong ethical and efficiency reasons for taxing it. A throughput tax is not the same as a rent tax but its incidence will partly fall on rent from unproduced resources extracted from the land. A throughput tax has some of the equity appeal of Henry George's rent tax on land. However, like all consumption taxes, it is regressive. This could be counteracted by retaining the income tax at the extremes – a posiive income tax for high incomes, a negative income tax for very low incomes, and a negligible income tax between the extremes. The essential idea is to gradually shift much of the tax burden away from "goods" like income and labor and toward "bads" like ecological damages and consumption of non-renewable resources. Such a shift would encourage resource-saving technologies, and should simultaneously improve both employment and ecological sustainability.

Of the three major goals of economic policy (sustainable scale, efficient allocation, and just distribution) the ecological tax reform is primarily aimed at the first; contributes positively if non-optimally toward the second; and requires some supplement from an attenuated income tax structure to serve the third. These goals are discussed more fully in the following section.

Allocation, Distribution, and Scale

Although ecological tax reform uses price as the policy instrument (price plus tax), the major goal is to limit quantity of throughput to a sustainable scale. A secondary goal is to raise public revenue. In practice, one should begin with an acceptable quantity of throughput in mind, and set the tax so as to likely result in that quantity. That tax would then represent a rough internalization of the previously externalized cost of excessive scale. If the tax bears on resource use in general then there will not be much room to avoid the tax by substitution, and resource demand will be inelastic, so revenue raised will be large. If the tax is aimed at inducing substitution away from the taxed activity (e.g., emissions of toxic wastes) then there will be a trade-off between revenue raised and success in inducing substitution. As with the present tax system, some fine-tuning would be required from time to time.

The relation among the three goals is clearest in the design of tradable permits schemes. These utilize a socially and ecologically set limit to the total annual depletion or pollution in a given area or sector of the economy. The right, say, to pollute was previously a free good because it was unlimited. With limits it becomes an economic asset. Who owns the new asset? It could be anyone, but it is best to vest ownership in the government and require firms to purchase the rights at auction from the government. The scarcity rents arising from scale limits are thus captured by the society as a whole and become public revenue. Once purchased, these permits can be freely traded among firms. Sustainable scale is served by the limited aggregate number of permits. Equitable distribution is served by initial public ownership of the new asset. Efficient allocation is served by allowing exchange of the new asset among firms.

Once an overall throughput scale limit is fixed as a social goal, one can thus fix that right quantity directly and let the market indirectly determine the corresponding right price. It is also possible to set the price (tax) directly and allow the market to find the corresponding right quantity. In both cases the target is the right quantity, and the "right" price is the price that leads the market to that quantity. Both procedures assume that there is a strong social preference for a sustainable aggregate scale, and that a market directed only by individualistic preferences and maximizing behavior cannot incorporate that social value.

The great virtue of the tradable permits scheme is that it forces us to distinguish three separate policy goals and to recognize that they require three separate policy instruments. The goals are:

(1) *Allocation* – the division of the resource flow among alternative product uses;

(2) *Distribution* – the division of the resource flow, embodied in products, among different people;

(3) *Scale* – the total volume of the resource flow, the matter-energy throughput taken from the environment as low-entropy resources and returned to the environment as high-entropy wastes. Scale is relative to environmental carrying capacity.

Economic theory tells us that relative prices formed by supply and demand in competitive markets lead to an efficient allocation. Economic theory also tells us that there is a different efficient allocation for every initial distribution of ownership, so that justice or fairness of distribution is a separate goal from efficiency and requires use of separate policy instruments – transfer payments such as welfare, social insurance, inheritance taxes, etc. As for scale, it is largely ignored by standard economic theory, which has implicitly assumed that environmental sources and sinks were infinite. Consequently there is in traditional economic theory no policy instrument for keeping scale within carrying capacity – nothing analogous to the Plimsoll line or load limit mark on a ship.

The scale limit, the economic Plimsoll line, is evolving in practice ahead of theory. The beauty of the tradable permits scheme is that, first, the society must face the scale question and draw a Plimsoll line at the amount of aggregate pollution (or depletion) that is ecologically sustainable. Second, rights to pollute (or deplete) up to that limited amount become a valuable asset and their ownership must be initially distributed in some politically acceptable manner. Only after these two political steps can market trading attain the efficient allocation. The market is "free" only after its ecological and distributional boundaries have been politically established.

The distribution and scale questions are just as "economic" as the allocation question, in that they all involve the comparison of costs and benefits. But the dimensions in which costs and benefits are defined are different in each of the three cases. Allocative prices cannot measure the costs and benefits of scale expansion, nor can they measure the costs and benefits of a more equal distribution of wealth. The three different optima require three different policy instruments. In each case an optimum is formally defined by the equality of falling marginal benefits and rising marginal costs. But the definitions and measures of costs and benefits in each of the three cases are different because the problems to whose solution they are instrumental are different. The relative price of shoes and bicycles suffices to allocate resources efficiently between shoes and bicycles, but is clearly not sufficient for deciding the proper range of inequality in wealth, nor for deciding how many people consuming how much per capita of natural resources gives the optimal scale relative to the ecosystem.

Distribution and scale involve relationships with the poor, the future, and other species, that are more social than individual in nature. *Homo economicus*, whether the self-contained atom of methodological individualism or the pure social automaton of collectivist ideology, is in either case a severe abstraction. Our concrete experience is that of "persons in community." We are individual persons, but our individual identity is defined by our social relations. Our relations to each other are not just external, they are also internal – i.e., the nature of the related entities (ourselves in this case) changes when relations among them change. We are related not only by the external nexus of individual willingnesses to pay for different things, but also by relations of kinship, friendship, citizenship, and trusteeship for the poor, the future, and for other species. The attempt to abstract from all these relationships a *Homo economicus*, whose identity is constituted only by individualistic willingness to pay, is a gross oversimplification of our concrete experience as persons in community – an example of what A. N. Whitehead called the "fallacy of misplaced concreteness."

The prices that measure the opportunity costs of reallocation are unrelated to measures of the opportunity costs of redistribution, or of a change in scale. Any trade-off among the three goals (e.g., an improvement in distribution in exchange for a worsening in scale or allocation, or more efficient allocation resulting from the harsher incentives of a less equal distribution of income), involves an ethical judgment about the quality of our social relations, rather than a supposedly simple willingness-to-pay calculation. The contrary view, that this choice among the three separate policy goals, and consequently the social relations that help to define us as persons, should be made on the basis of individual willingness to pay, just as the allocative trade-off between chewing gum and shoelaces is made, seems to be dominant in economics today. It is part of the retrograde contemporary reduction of all ethical choice to the level of personal tastes weighted by income.

The omission of the scale of the macroeconomy from economic

theory has several explanations. The most obvious is that when the theory was first devised, the scale of the economic subsystem was small relative to the environment; the world was "empty," so it seemed reasonable to treat the environment as a free good. Those days are clearly past, and we now live in a relatively "full" world. The second explanation is more complicated. Basically it is the doctrine that all we consume is value added, and all value added is the product of the human agents of labor and capital. This notion is examined in the following section.

Consumption and Value Added

When we speak of consumption, what is it that we think of as being consumed? Alfred Marshall reminded us of the laws of conservation of matter/energy and the consequent impossibility of consuming the material building blocks of commodities:

> Man cannot create material things – his efforts and sacrifices result in changing the form or arrangement of matter to adapt it better for the satisfaction of his wants – as his production of material products is really nothing more than a rearrangement of matter which gives it new utilities, so his consumption of them is nothing more than a disarrangement of matter which destroys its utilities. (Marshall, 1961, pp. 63–64.)

What we destroy or consume in consumption according to this view is the improbable arrangements of those building blocks, arrangements that give utility for humans, arrangements that were made by humans for human purposes. This utility added to matter/energy by human action is not production in the sense of creation of matter/energy, which is just as impossible as its destruction by consumption. Useful structure is added to matter/energy (natural resource flows) by the agency of labor and capital stocks. The value of this useful structure imparted by labor and capital is what economists call "value added." This value added is all that is "consumed," i.e., used up in consumption. New value needs to be added again by the agency of labor and capital before it can be consumed again. That to which value is being added is the flow of natural resources, conceived ultimately as the indestructible building blocks of nature. The value consumed by humans is, in this view, no greater than the value added by humans, which in turn is equal to the sum of all value added. In this standard economist's vision we consume only that value which we added in the first place. And then we add it again, and consume

116

it again, etc. This vision is formalized in the famous diagram of the isolated circular flow of value between firms (production) and households (consumption) found in the initial pages of every economics textbook.

With all this focus on value added one would think that there would be some discussion of *that to which value is being added*. But modern economists say no more about it than Marshall. It is just "matter," and its properties are not very interesting to economists. In fact they are becoming ever less interesting to economists as science uncovers their basic uniformity. As Barnett and Morse (1963) put it:

> Advances in fundamental science have made it possible to take advantage of the uniformity of matter/energy – a uniformity that makes it feasible, without preassignable limit, to escape the quantitative constraints imposed by the character of the earth's crust.

In such a view, that to which value is being added are merely homogeneous, indestructible building blocks – atoms in the original sense – of which there is no conceivable scarcity. That to which value is added is therefore inert, undifferentiated, interchangeable, and superabundant – very dull stuff indeed, compared to the value-adding agents of labor with all its human capacities and capital that embodies the marvels of human knowledge. It is not surprising that value added is the centerpiece of economic accounting, and that the presumably passive stuff to which value is added has received minimal attention. (Daly and Cobb, 1994, Chap. 10)

Three examples will show how little attention is given to that to which value is added, which for brevity I will refer to as "resources." Some Philistines ("noneconomists" as they are now called) have questioned whether there are enough resources in the world for everyone to use them at the rate Americans do. This ignorant fear is put to rest by Professor Lester Thurow (1980, p. 118), who points out that the question assumes that the "rest of the world is going to achieve the consumption standards of the average American without at the same time achieving the productivity standards of the average American. This of course is algebraically impossible. The world can consume only what it can produce."

In this comforting view, you can only disarrange matter (consume) if you have previously arranged it (produced). Resources are totally passive recipients of form added by labor and capital. Value added is everything, and it is impossible to subtract value that was never added. So if you are consuming something you must have produced

117

it, either recently or in the past. More and more high-consuming people just means more and more value was added. Where else could the arrangements of matter have come from? It is "algebraically impossible" for consumption to exceed value added – at least in the economist's tight little abstract world of the circular flow of exchange value.

A second example comes from Professor William Nordhaus (1991), who said that global warming would have only a small effect on the U.S. economy because basically only agriculture is sensitive to climate, and agriculture is only three per cent of total value added, of GNP. In this perspective, it is solely the value added to seeds, soil, sunlight, and rainfall by labor and capital that keeps us alive. Older economists might have asked about what happens to marginal utility, price, and the percentage of GNP going to food when food becomes very scarce, say, due to a drought? What about the inelasticity of demand for necessities? Could not the three percent of GNP accounted for by agriculture easily rise to ninety per cent during a famine? But these currently unfashionable considerations give mere stuff a more than passive role in value, and diminish the dogmatic monopoly of value added by human agents of labor and capital.

The importance of mere stuff is frequently downplayed by pointing out that the entire extractive sector accounts for a mere five or six per cent of GNP. But if in reality the ninety-five per cent of value added is not independent of the five per cent in the extractive sector, but rather depends upon it – is based on it – then the impression of relative unimportance is false. The image this conjures in my mind is that of an inverted pyramid balanced on its point. The five or six per cent of the volume of the pyramid near the point on which it is resting represents the GNP from the extractive sector. The rest of the pyramid is value added to extracted resources. That five per cent is the base on which the other ninety-five per cent rests: that to which its value is added. Value cannot be added to nothing. Adding value is more like multiplication than addition – we multiply the value of stuff by labor and capital. But multiplying by zero always gives zero.

Indeed, since the value of the extracted resources themselves (the five or six per cent of GNP) represents mostly value added in extraction and processing, practically the entire pyramid of value added is resting on a tiny point of near zero dimension representing the *in situ* value of the resources (user cost). This image of a growing and tottering pyramid makes me want to stop thinking exclusively about value added and think some more about that to which value is being added. What, exactly, is holding up this pyramid of value added?

A third example comes from the theory of production and the customary use of a multiplicative form for the production function, the most popular being the Cobb-Douglas. Frequently production is treated as a function of capital and labor alone – resources are omitted entirely. But now economists have taken to including resources. However, the welcome step toward realism thus taken is very small, because, although resources are now admitted to be necessary for production, the amount of resources needed for any given level of output can become arbitrarily small, approaching zero, as long as capital or labor are substituted in sufficient quantities. Georgescu-Roegen referred to this "paper and pencil exercise" as Solow's and Stiglitz's "conjuring trick."*

---

*N. Georgescu-Roegen deserves to be quoted at length on this point because so few people have understood it. He writes the "Solow-Stiglitz variant" of the Cobb-Douglas function as:

$$Q = K^{a_1} R^{a_2} L^{a_3} \tag{1}$$

"where Q is output, K is the stock of capital, R is the flow of natural resources used in production, L is the labor supply, and $a_1 + a_2 + a_3 = 1$ and of course, $a_i > 0$.

From this formula it follows that with a constant labor power, L_0, one could obtain any Q_0, if the flow of natural resources satisfies the condition

$$R^{a_2} = \frac{Q_0}{K^{a_1} L_0^{a_3}} \tag{2}$$

This shows that R may be as small as we wish, provided K is sufficiently large. *Ergo*, we can obtain a constant annual product indefinitely even from a very small stock of resources $R > 0$, if we decompose R into an infinite series $R = \sum R_i$, with $R_i \to 0$, use R_i in year i, and increase the stock of capital each year as required by (2). But this *ergo* is not valid in actuality. In actuality, the increase of capital implies an additional depletion of resources. And if $K \to \inf$, the R will rapidly be exhausted by the production of capital. Solow and Stiglitz could not have come out with their conjuring trick had they borne in mind, first, that any material process consists in the transformation of some materials into others (the flow elements) by some agents (the fund elements), and second, that natural resources are the very sap of the economic process. They are *not* just like any other production factor. A change in capital or labor can only diminish the amount of waste in the production of a commodity: no agent can create the material on which it works. Nor can capital create the stuff out of which it is made. In some cases it may also be that the same service can be provided by a design that requires less matter or energy. But even in this direction there exists a limit, unless we believe that the ultimate fate of the economic process is an earthly Garden of Eden.

"The question that confronts us today is whether we are going to discover new sources of energy that can be safely used. No elasticities of some Cobb-Douglas function can help us to answer it."

(N. Georgescu-Roegen, "Comments ..." in V. Kerry Smith, ed., *Scarcity and Growth Reconsidered*, Baltimore: Resources for the Future and Johns Hopkins University Press, 1979, p. 98.)

Policy Implications

A fundamental economic principle is to maximize the productivity of the limiting factor in the short run and to invest in its increase in the long run. If factors are good substitutes, then the absence of one does not limit the usefulness of the other – i.e. neither can be limiting. But if they are complements, then the one in short supply is limiting. For example, plant growth requires sunlight, soil, and water. These factors are complements, not substitutes. Extra sunlight does not compensate for a lack of water. Plant growth is effectively limited by whichever of the three factors is most scarce. Unless that limiting factor is increased, it does no good to increase the others. The idea is familiar to ecologists and chemists as Liebig's Law of the Minimum.

From the foregoing it is clear that the relationship between value-adding agents (man-made capital, including labor power) and that to which value is added, natural resources (the natural income flow produced by the stock of natural capital), is one of complementarity. Even if man-made and natural capital were good, but imperfect, substitutes, the process of transforming the latter into the former would still reach an optimum extent. But if man-made and natural capital are complements, that optimum extent will be reached much sooner and more dramatically, since the scarcity of the factor in shortest supply will limit the usefulness of the other, more abundant factor. In the empty-world economy of the past, man-made capital was the limiting factor. In today's full-world economy it is remaining natural capital that is scarce and therefore limiting. The fish catch is limited not by the number of fishing boats, but by the remaining populations of fish in the sea. The timber harvest is limited not by the number of sawmills or lumberjacks, but by the remaining standing forests and our desire to preserve the non-timber services of forests (wildlife habitat, flood control, recreation, etc.).

As we move into an era in which natural capital is limiting, we need to economize on it more. That means its price must go up relative to man-made capital. But since much natural capital is common property, outside the market, and since the market itself is very short-sighted temporally, it is necessary to raise the price of natural capital by public policy. As we have seen earlier, this can be done in a general way by shifting the tax base from value added (labor and capital are no longer limiting) on to that to which value is added (the natural resource flow yielded by natural capital). In short, tax throughput, not income.

Consumption limits will be set by differing *national* policies – not by a single global policy. Nations could limit their total consumption (scale) by a strategy of low population and high per capita consumption or by a strategy of high population and low per capita consumption. Different nations will make different choices. Some will not even limit aggregate consumption and those that do will make different choices regarding per capita consumption vs. population. These differences cannot be maintained in a world of free trade, free capital mobility, and increasingly free (or uncontrolled) migration. Compensating tariffs will be necessary to keep these national differences from being homogenized. National policies of controlling consumption and population, and of counting external costs, are more important to sound allocation, distribution, and scale than are the tenuous gains from comparative advantage and free trade, which are currently celebrated beyond reason. This argument does not imply autarchy, but it does throw cold water on the faddish advocacy of global economic integration and consequent homogenization of policies as an unquestioned good. "Globalization" ranks with "the demographic transition" and "dematerialization" as a false panacea – another germ of truth that has been allowed to grow into a whale of a fantasy in order to protect the dominant myth of our culture: that of an ever-growing economy.

Two views of production have been discussed: (a) only value added to indestructible building blocks is consumed, vs. (b) value added by nature as well as human agents is also consumed. There are important policy differences implied by each.

(a) The value-added view of wealth would lead one to reject the very notion of a "global pie" of wealth to be divided justly or unjustly among nations and people. In this view, there is no pie – there are only a lot of separate tarts which some statistician has stupidly aggregated into an abstract pie. The separate tarts are the product solely of value added by the labor and capital of the nations that produced them. If nation A is asked to share some of its large tart with nation B who baked a small tart, the appeal should be made to nation A's generosity and not to any notion of distributive justice, much less exploitation. On the assumption that all value comes from labor and capital, and that nature contributes only a material substratum which is indestructible and superabundant, and hence value-less, this is a quite reasonable view. Are you poor? Well, just add more value by your own labor and capital. There are no limits from nature. Stop whining about this imaginary pie, and get busy adding value. This view is common among neoclassical economists. And if we accept its presuppositions it is not unreasonable.

(b) The natural capital view can reject the imaginary pie also, and look at the tarts different people have baked. Are they really only the product of labor and capital and random atoms? Certainly not. You need flour and sugar and butter and apples. Before that you needed wheat, sugar cane, milk, and apple trees. And before that you needed a gene pool for wheat, sugar cane, cows, and apples, with some minimal degree of genetic diversity, and grass growing on soil whose fertility is maintained by all sorts of worms and microbes, and sunlight without too much ultraviolet, and rainfall that is not too acidic, and catchment areas to keep that rain from eroding topsoil, and predictable seasonal temperatures regulated by the mix of gasses in an atmosphere without too much CO_2, etc., etc. In other words, we need natural capital and the flow of resources and services that it renders – a whole lot more than indestructible building blocks! Our dowry of natural capital is more or less given, and is not the product of human labor and ingenuity. It is in many ways systemic and indivisible – more like a vast pie than separate tarts. How it is stewarded and distributed is not an idle question based on some gratuitous aggregation. The demands of justice impinge strongly on the stewardship and distribution of the common life-supporting exosomatic organs we refer to as natural capital, but very little on value added, since the latter rather naturally and reasonably belongs to whoever added it.

A North/South bargain will have to be struck in which the South gets very serious about limiting fertility (and the over-consumption of its elites), while the North gets very serious about limiting over-consumption (and the poverty-reinforcing high fertility of its marginalized underclass). But the North will not get serious about limiting consumption as long as our leaders remain convinced by our economists' view that all wealth comes from value added, that we can only consume what we have produced. We have to recognize that we can and do consume a lot more than we produce, and that what we consume over and above conventional value added is value added by nature. But in addition to consuming value added by nature we are now consuming the very capacity of nature to add value in the future, i.e., natural capital.

Also, in the absence of a North/South bargain not much is likely to happen on either population or consumption. Why should the South control its overpopulation if the resources saved thereby are merely gobbled up by Northern over-consumption? Why should the North control its over-consumption if the saved resources will merely allow a larger number of poor people to subsist at the same level of misery in the South?

The policy implications for the North are that we must economize on and invest in natural capital, because it has become the limiting factor (replacing man-made capital in that role) as we have moved from an empty world to a full world. To force ourselves to economize on natural capital we must raise its price above the market level. A concrete method of accomplishing this is ecological tax reform. Viewed in a North/South context, ecological tax reform takes on even greater relevance as the North's best contribution to a global bargain.

Conclusions

Since our consumption uses up value added by nature, as well as by human agents, the scale of the macroeconomy must respect the rate at which nature "adds value" – i.e., the rate at which resources can be regenerated and wastes can be absorbed. Ecological tax reform can make scale more sustainable, allocation more efficient, and distribution more equitable.

We are consuming natural value added, converting raw materials into waste, depleting and polluting, faster than nature can absorb the pollutants and regenerate the resources. Economists who tell us not to worry because it is algebraically impossible for us to consume more value than we added have studied too much algebra and not enough biology and physics. Consumption – that is, the transformation of natural capital into man-made capital and then ultimately into waste – cannot escape the basic question of what is the sustainable scale of this transformation. What is the optimal scale of the economic subsystem, the scale beyond which further conversion of natural into man-made capital costs us more (in terms of natural capital services lost) than it benefits us (in terms of man-made capital services gained)? Growing beyond the optimum is by definition anti-economic. Currently growth appears anti-economic, as indicated by the rate of consumption of natural capital and the deterioration of community associated with growth's requirements for mobility. The future path of progress therefore is not growth, but development – not an increase in throughput, but increases in efficiency.

Individual nations, not the globe, will control consumption by limiting both population and per capita consumption. Different national strategies for limiting total national consumption cannot coexist in an integrated world economy dominated by free trade, free capital mobility, and free migration. The use of tariffs and a general backing away from global integration toward relative self-sufficiency will be necessary. But a global North/South compact among nations will be needed to limit over-consumption and overpopulation.

References

Barnett, Harold and Chandler Morse. *Scarcity and Growth.* Baltimore: Johns Hopkins University Press. 1963.

Costanza, R. "Three General Policies to Achieve Sustainability" in A. M. Jansson, M. Hammer, C. Folke, and R. Costanza (eds). *Investing in Natural Capital: The Ecological Economics Approach to Sustainability.* Washington DC: Island Press. 1994. pp. 392–407.

Costanza, R. and H. E. Daly. "Natural Capital and Sustainable Development," *Conservation Biology.* No. 6, pp. 37–46. 1992.

Daly, Herman E. *Steady-State Economics.* Washington DC: Island Press. 2nd ed., 1991.

Daly, H. and J. Cobb. *For the Common Good,* Boston: Beacon Press. 2nd ed., 1994.

Georgescu-Roegen, Nicholas. "Comments ..." in V. Kerry Smith, ed., *Scarcity and Growth Reconsidered,* Baltimore: Resources for the Future and Johns Hopkins University Press. 1979. p. 98.

Hawken, Paul. *The Ecology of Commerce: A Declaration of Sustainability.* New York: Harper Business. 1993.

Marshall, Alfred. *Principles of Economics.* New York: Macmillan. 9th ed., 1961 (originally 1920).

Nordhaus, William. Quoted in "Academy Panel Split on Greenhouse Adaptation." *Science.* September 13, 1991. p. 1206.

———. *Science.* October 18, 1981. p. 358. "Ecological Economics" (letter).

Oates, Wallace E. "Pollution Charges as a Source of Public Revenues." Working Paper No. 91-22, University of Maryland, Department of Economics. 1991.

Page, Talbot. *Conservation and Economic Efficiency.* Baltimore: Johns Hopkins University Press. 1977.

Passell, P. "Cheapest Protection of Nature May Lie in Taxes, Not Laws." *New York Times,* Nov. 24, 1992.

Repetto, R., R. C. Dower, R. Jenkins, and J. Geoghegan. *Green Fees: How A Tax Shift Can Work for the Government and Economy.* Washington, DC: World Resources Institute. 1992.

Thurow, Lester. *The Zero-Sum Society.* New York: Penguin Books. 1980.

von Weizsäcker, E. U. and J. Jesinghaus. *Ecological Tax Reform: A Policy Proposal for Sustainable Development.* London: Zed Books. 1992.

World Bank, "Development and the Environment," *World Development Report.* Figure 3.2, p. 69. Washington DC and New York: World Bank and Oxford University Press. 1992.

9

New Concepts of Fiduciary Responsibility

Edward Tasch and Stephen Viederman

As long as an ecological tax reform of the kind discussed in the previous chapter is not put into practice, moving toward sustainability will require ingenious and courageous management strategies because of the inherent tension between economics, as currently practiced, and ecology. When this tension is felt in the business world, most executives tend to choose short-term economic advantage over long-term ecological sustainabiliy, and to justify their choice they frequently evoke the principle of fiduciary responsibility. This argument has again and again been used as the last line of defense in discussions between environmentalists and corporate executives.

The concept of fiduciary responsibility has been based on a narrow notion of financial prudence. An institutional investment manager quoted in the following pages put it succinctly: "As a fiduciary, I have a moral obligation to my investors to maximize return and minimize risk. I simply cannot take into account exogenous factors like social or environmental impact."

In this chapter, Stephen Viederman and Edward Tasch, two top executives of the Jessie Smith Noyes Foundation, argue that new notions of prudence and fiduciary responsibility are developing in the investment community which include concern for the impact of commercial activity on the environment and on local communities. Both authors are well placed to observe these changes, as they are also executives of environmental organizations, Viederman being a Director of the Rainforest Foundation and Tasch a Director of CERES, the Coalition for Environmentally Responsible Economies.

After reviewing the recent impressive growth of the social investment movement, which now influences investment decisions involving billions of dollars by making ecological sustainability an explicit investment criterion, the authors provide an illuminating analysis of the values and practices of their foundation. They point out that among financial institutions, most foundations are in a very curious, self-contradictory position because of an "iron curtain" between their endowment management and grant-making programs. The Jessie Smith Noyes Foundation, by contrast, has come to view its assets as well as its income as tools for social change.

The authors describe in some detail what this means in practice in terms of the management of their assets and the education of their grantees. What emerges from this description is an expanded sense of prudence and fiduciary responsibility, grounded in ecological literacy and concern for future generations.

Rate of return, liquidity, diversification, emerging markets, hedging, derivatives, asset allocation: the business of today's institutional asset manager seems as remote from global warming and ozone holes as mahjongg is from gene mapping.

The notion that financial institutions might play a role in steering business toward sustainability is, to be sure, quixotic. To most financiers, it is downright wrongheaded. Consider, for example, the remarks of two contemporary financiers, whose views are more the norm than the exception. The first, a noted Wall Street investment banker who is also widely known for his environmental interests, gave a 1990 commencement address about lessons learned from the Exxon Valdez spill, after which he took questions from the audience:

Q. You have spoken eloquently about corporate responsibility and the need for better federal regulation, but you have said nothing about the role of Wall Street. Don't investment banks and financial institutions have a role to play in shaping corporate policy, in transmitting investors' concerns regarding the environmental impact of corporate activity?

A. Absolutely not. One of the cornerstones of free markets is efficient capital markets. It would be inappropriate, inefficient, or worse to attempt to layer concerns about environmental impact onto financial intermediaries, who are singularly focussed on the task of providing corporate access to capital on the best possible terms and upon whom the efficient functioning of capital markets depends.

The second institutional investment manager, responsible for many hundreds of millions of dollars of institutional venture capital portfolios, made the following remarks during a conversation:

As a fiduciary, I have a moral obligation to my investors to maximize return and minimize risk. I simply cannot take into account exogenous factors like social or environmental impact, or I will reduce the opportunity set and thereby reduce the rate of return.

Such constructs of the roles and obligations of financial intermediaries and fiduciaries have arisen with a certain inevitability over the past two hundred years, ever since Adam Smith originally formulated the concept of an "invisible hand" through which each man striving only to better himself would, through a thriving free market economy, improve standards of living for all. After tracing how these views have developed and their context in contemporary financial markets, we will describe how one small financial institution, the Jessie Smith Noyes Foundation, is trying to construct for itself a new definition of fiduciary responsibility.

The Prudent Man

In 1830, a Massachusetts court offered a definition of prudence that has, through decades of subsequent re-examination and re-definition, survived in the canon of fiduciary responsibility as "the prudent man rule":

All that can be required of a trustee to invest is, that he shall conduct himself faithfully and exercise sound discretion. He is to observe how men of prudence, discretion and intelligence manage their own affairs, not in regard to speculation, but in regard to the permanent disposition of their funds, considering probable income, as well as the probable safety of the capital to be invested.[1]

This describes a narrow form of "sustainability," which persists among fiduciaries today: sustainability as maintenance and growth of financial capital, sustainability as growth of assets sufficient to keep pace with inflation and preserve or even augment purchasing power. The concept of prudence, built around risk aversion, predictability of income and preservation of capital, came to define a whole culture of

[1] Longstreth, Bevis. *Modern Investment Management and the Prudent Man Rule.* New York: Oxford University Press, 1986, p. 12.

managing "other people's money." In the mid-nineteenth century, such a definition of sustainability was understandably devoid of a whole range of concerns which had yet to be articulated. But in the late twentieth century, our knowledge regarding environmental degradation and the social problems which persist in the wake of economic growth and rising standards of living should impel us to ask the following questions:

- Can there be fiduciary responsibility *without* incorporating questions about the social and environmental impacts of economic growth?
- How do concepts of fiduciary responsibility affect corporate culture?
- What is the relationship between fiduciary responsibility and institutional or corporate responsibility?
- Can institutional investment management be an effective agent for change?

Sustainability, as maintenance or restoration of ecological integrity, provision of economic security, and protection of popular participation in the life of a community, takes on a new meaning.

The Question of Scale

The contemporary fiduciary cannot easily factor such issues into his/her decision-making, due in part to the very scale of modern financial institutions and their role in global capital markets.

Consider the following items, which evidence the staggering growth of financial institutions and capital markets:

- Private pension fund assets in the United States grew from about $250 billion in 1975 to $2.5 trillion in 1994.
- The State of California's public employee pension fund grew from $13.3 billion in 1979 to $80 billion in 1994.
- In 1990, nearly a hundred portfolio management organizations managed more than $10 billion, and the ten largest managed $800 billion of financial assets of the roughly $5 trillion in stocks, bonds and real estate owned by institutions.
- Volume on the New York Stock Exchange increased from 767 million shares in 1960 to almost 36 billion shares in 1986 and to the 70 billion range in 1993. From 1982 to 1992, trading increased tenfold in Tokyo, twelvefold in Frankfurt and thirtyfold in London.
- In 1960, annual turnover (shares traded as a percentage of total tradeable shares outstanding) on the New York Stock Exchange

was 12 percent. Turnover rose to 64 percent in 1986, but when the activity which now occurs on regional exchanges, in the over-the-counter market and in foreign markets is taken into account, the consolidated trading in Exchange-listed stocks in the U.S. and abroad produced a turnover of 87 percent.

- Derivatives and synthetics – futures, warrants, swaps and scores of newly engineered financial products – have created multi-trillion-dollar markets, many of which have doubled in a single year. In 1992, the value of swap contracts equaled the combined worth of the New York and Tokyo stock markets. Annual international volume of equity index derivatives in 1992 exceeded $10 trillion.
- Pre-tax profits of U.S. brokers and investment banks reached a record $8.9 billion in 1993.

As financial markets explode, intermediaries and transaction-based incentives increasingly influence corporate decision-making and the flow of capital. Increasing complexity of financial instruments and global markets drives increasing specialization of financial managers. Fiduciaries seem more removed than ever from the social and environment consequences of their decisions. "Most of the time," writes leading investment banker Felix Rohatyn, "the product being bought or sold only exists on a computer screen or as an electronic impulse on a magnetic tape.... The movements of capital and the paper economy related to it used to be the result of industrial and commercial activity; now they are the cause."[2]

When transactions come first, the consequences on individuals and community can be devastating. Commentator Adam Smith describes how most financiers never see the effects of their decision-making:

A worker may work for the same company for twenty years. A manager may live in the community, support its schools, and work to integrate the company and the community. But the owner reigns supreme; it is up to him whether the plant is shut down, the worker laid off, the manager sent somewhere else. Yet the owner these days is seldom the founder with the big house up on the hill. Technically, the owner (or at least one of the owners) is probably a pension fund or mutual fund, represented by a young portfolio manager who shares neither history nor loyalty with the company and who will sell out in five minutes if that will improve his track record. Or the owner may even be a group of arbitrageurs seeking the fastest return possible on a very swift turnover – measured in hours, not in months or years.[3]

---

[2] Rohatyn, Felix. "Ethics in America's Money Culture." *New York Times,* June 3, 1987.
[3] Smith, Adam. *The Roaring '80s,* New York: Viking Penguin, 1988, p. 271.

The implications for those concerned with the social and environmental impact of business are daunting. Whither, amidst the torrent of financial activity and the divorce of portfolio managers from people and places affected by their decisions, the concept of sustainability?

Asset Management and the Behavior of Business

So long as assets are viewed as passive pools of income-generating securities, fiduciary responsibility ends with a diversified asset allocation plan and the selection and monitoring of money managers. Yet some institutional investors have taken in recent years a first step towards a more proactive definition of fiduciary responsibility, one which recognizes that their investment expectations can and do impact corporate behavior.

The Council of Institutional Investors, whose membership includes roughly eighty of the nation's largest public employee and union pension funds, focuses attention on corporate governance and the problem of boards of directors failing to adequately represent the financial interests of shareholders. In particular, the Council has vigorously attacked distorted compensation packages for senior management of many corporations: "High pay is not the same as pay for performance and may not, in fact, improve performance," noted the Council's April, 1994 newsletter. "Compensation can be tied to performance without giving away the store. And giving away the store pursuant to a formula still leaves one without a store."

The California Public Employees Retirement System (CALPERS), one of the nation's largest institutional investors and an active Council member, has been a leader on issues of corporate governance. Most recently CALPERS has included issues of workplace conditions and employment practices in their annual governance reviews as "one of many other considerations ... in our investment decisions."[4]

Such initiatives mark the beginning of a process of integrating into investment decision-making factors that have previously been considered beyond the purview of financial analysis. How does a $10 million CEO compensation package affect employee morale? How does a CEO's "independent wealth" affect his/her attitude toward and loyalty to the corporation? Will directors who are paid $40,000

[4] St. Goar, Jinny, "CALPERS Weighs In," *Plan Sponsor*, September, 1994, pp. 40–41.

per annum in fees act with sufficient independence to effectively oversee senior management? Will corporations with broader employee participation in ownership or decision-making enjoy a competitive advantage? These are questions about compensation and governance, specifically, and, more generally, about corporate culture.

Assistant Secretary of Labor Olena Berg, the former Chief Deputy Treasurer of California who currently oversees the regulation of the U.S. pension industry, believes that a broader view of investor responsibility is inevitable for pension funds. "We will be asking pension funds to change their thinking," Berg says. "Instead of thinking only about beating the market by another increment, we want them to think about how their investments are contributing to the long-run health of the economy ... Given the size of the funds, it doesn't make sense to try to beat the market for a quarter. When you are the market, as the funds are, you can't beat it. The goal should be an overall lifting of the economic boats by investing in ways that are economically productive and create more and better jobs." (*New York Times,* August 10, 1993.)

The role of financial institutions in steering business toward sustainability begins with such steps. Concerns about corporate governance and the creations of long-term benefits to the economy as a whole mark evolving concepts of "prudence" towards broader investor responsibility and the inclusion in investment decision-making of factors previously beyond the purview of financial analysis.

Nevertheless, the connection between the long-term health of the economy and the social and environmental costs of economic growth remains problematic for fiduciaries. Institutional investors have been very slow to embrace "social investing," or strategies which explicitly seek to address this connection.

Social Investing

Social investing, or "ethical investing" as it is called in England, is the term that has come to be used to describe investment strategies which take into account social and environmental impact alongside financial performance. It is not a precise term. As a result it is difficult to be certain of the scale of the endeavor. *The Economist* (September 3, 1994) suggests that there is "an estimated $650 billion now managed according to some ethical guidelines," but that figure is probably an overestimate.

131

FIGURE 1

UNITED STATES TRUST COMPANY BOSTON
Investment Management

ENVIRONMENTAL SCREENS

WE SEEK COMPANIES WHICH HAVE:
+ CONSISTENTLY GOOD COMPLIANCE RECORDS
+ CLEAR ENVIRONMENTAL POLICIES
+ A CHAIN OF RESPONSIBILITY FROM TOP MANAGEMENT FOR ENVIRONMENTAL PROGRAMS
+ INNOVATIVE POLLUTION CONTROL PROGRAMS
+ MADE SIGNIFICANT PROGRESS IN REDUCING WASTE AND EMISSIONS AT THE SOURCE, ENERGY CONSERVATION, AND/ OR RECYCLING OF WASTE MATERIALS
+ REGULAR ENVIRONMENTAL AND ENERGY AUDITS
+ STRONG EMERGENCY RESPONSE SYSTEMS
+ PRODUCTS OR SERVICES THAT HELP SOLVE ENVIRONMEN-TAL PROBLEMS
+ POSITIVE RESPONSES TO THE CERES PRINCIPLES

WE AVOID COMPANIES THAT:
− PARTICIPATE IN THE NUCLEAR POWER INDUSTRY, MANU-FACTURE PESTICIDES OR OTHER AGRICULTURAL CHEM-ICALS, ENGAGE IN AGRICULTURAL BIOTECHNOLOGY
− SHOW PATTERNS OF ENVIRONMENTAL VIOLATIONS, UNLESS COMPANY HAS MADE A MAJOR COMMITMENT TO SOLVING COMPLIANCE PROBLEMS
− HAVE BEEN NEGLIGENT IN HANDLING ENVIRONMENTAL PROBLEMS, UNLESS COMPANY IS SUFFICIENTLY INVOLVED IN CORRECTING PROBLEMS
− ARE RESPONSIBLE FOR MAJOR ENVIRONMENTAL DISAS-TERS, UNLESS COMPANY IS SUFFICIENTLY INVOLVED IN CORRECTING UNDERLYING CAUSES
− ARE UNCOOPERATIVE IN DISCLOSING ENVIRONMENTAL INFORMATION
− ARE IN "DIRTY" INDUSTRIES WITH BELOW-AVERAGE RECORDS OF PERFORMANCE
− USE UNNECESSARILY DAMAGING INPUTS WHERE OTHERS IN INDUSTRY ARE USING ALTERNATIVES

What is clear is that there has been significant growth in the field since 1981 when the Social Investment Forum, the trade association for social managers, was formed. It should be noted that individual investors are driving the growth of mutual funds with social investment strategies. There are an estimated 33 such funds (one-third of which were established during the last year), with total assets of $2.5 billion, reflecting a trebling since 1990.

While emphasis and specialization vary between investors and firms, a number of broad screens are illustrative of the types of criteria by which companies are evaluated by many social investment advisors:

- Environmental impact and performance
- Employee benefits or ownership
- Community involvement and charitable giving
- Racial and gender diversity of directors and management
- Limited or no weapons component manufacture
- Limited or no tobacco or alcohol production

One of the variables of social investing is how such screens are applied. An example of a general environmental screen, shown in Figure 1, indicates some of the complexity involved in screening. Some screens are "negative" – avoiding whole sectors or companies whose practices are not consistent with stated criteria. Others are "positive" – seeking companies demonstrating leadership in responsible business practices. Some are "relative," recognizing the best in class in industry sectors which as a whole remain problematic for social investors.

More often than not the investment program is passive: buying and selling stock, without companies having any awareness of the views of social investors except through their proxy voting.

Increasingly, however, initiating or actively supporting shareholder resolutions has afforded concerned investors a means by which their voice can be registered with corporate management. Organizations such as the Interfaith Center on Corporate Responsibility (ICCR) work actively with church pension funds to sponsor shareholder resolutions on a range of social investment concerns. Since 1971, ICCR has sponsored more than 5,000 resolutions, on matters ranging from the environment to South Africa, from infant formula abuses to equal employment opportunity, from wage levels in the *maquiladoras* of Mexico to economic conversion of weapons manufacturers.

The financial performance of social investment funds is a topic of continuing debate. Most institutional investors eschew social investment based upon two almost axiomatic premises:

- That the extra layer of "non-financial" factors will reduce the opportunity set, increase risk, and reduce return,
- That any investment that yields a financial return also produces social benefits, in terms of jobs and products or services that meet a need.

As evidence of the first premise, the underperformance of social investment portfolios over various periods is often cited by analysts; however, comparable periods of underperformance can be found in virtually every sector of the money management industry.

Discussions of social investment returns are muddied by the fact that there is significant evidence that most money managers – including, of course, those that employ no social or environmental screens – underperform market indices over time. For example, one study of 769 all-equity pension fund accounts with assets of more than $120 billion "found that on average the funds' annualized returns over each three-year interval ... lagged behind the S&P 500-stock index by 1 percentage point and by 2.1 percentage points when the funds' returns are weighted by size ... And that's not counting management fees or lower returns on cash holdings." (*Business Week,* July 13, 1992.) For this reason, index funds grew in popularity among institutional investors during the 1980s, with the percentage of institutional equities invested in index funds rising from less than 5 percent to approximately 25 percent. (*The Economist*, April 30, 1994.)

In 1990, the Domini Social Index became the first index fund to incorporate social and environmental screens. Since its inception, the Domini Index is up 71%, vs. a 60.5% increase for the S&P 500. For the nine years ending in 1993, the institutional equity accounts at Franklin Research and Development, an early leader in the field, yielded an annualized rate of return of 16.75, before fees, against an annualized S&P return of 15.35 over the same period. In the 13 years ending in December 1993, U.S. Trust yielded an annualized return of 15.1% before fees. In the three years ending on June 30, 1994, Winslow Management, a balanced manager focussing on environmental impact and innovation, achieved an annualized return of 10.17% before fees, against a balanced index weighted 65 percent S&P 500 and 35 percent in Lehman/Government Indexes, which for the 36 months was at 8.97 percent.

Economically Targeted Investing

While most financial institutions have been reluctant to pursue social investing through stock and fixed-income portfolios, some have, however, pursued "economically targeted investments" (ETIs) in their private or alternative investments. While lacking a single, standardized definition, ETIs have been defined by the Center for Policy Alternatives as "any prudent investment that fills a capital gap in an underfinanced area of the economy and earns a risk-adjusted market rate of return." Aiming to produce competitive returns and targeted social benefits, ETIs have included small business loans, venture funds dedicated to minority-owned businesses, and mortgage pools for low-cost housing.[5]

The Colorado Public Employees' Retirement Association (PERA) targets more than $850 million, or about six percent of its total assets, to economic development investments in Colorado. PERA invests $75 million through Colorado Housing and Finance Agency bonds to finance fixed-rate, long-term small business loans in Colorado. Since 1992, the California Public Employee Retirement System has committed $375 million for single-family housing construction when traditional financing sources withdrew from the market. By the end of FY 1992, CALPERS had invested $5.6 billion, or over seven percent of total assets of $77 billion, in investments classified as ETIs.

As of September, 1993, the twenty largest U.S. public pension funds had invested more than $23 billion in ETIs, with roughly 85 percent going to mortgage-related investments and the remainder in venture capital, private placements, or other direct investments.

Despite these initiatives, however, nine out of ten pension funds responding to a 1994 survey conducted by *Institutional Investor* magazine indicated that they felt ETIs were not consistent with their fiduciary responsibility to secure the greatest financial returns for their beneficiaries. Nearly three-quarters of survey respondents were corporate pension funds.

For those who have pursued ETIs, various financial and social measurements have been used to evaluate performance. Massachusetts measures its small-business-loan securities against 90-day Treasuries. The GE pension fund expects an economically targeted mezzanine fund to beat the S&P 500 by 300 basis points. As for social benefits, yardsticks include number of new homes under a certain price level or jobs created within a defined geographical area or within a particular population.

But questions regarding rate of return, performance benchmarks,

---

[5] Center for Policy Alternatives, "Rebuilding America's Communities," conference report, 1994.

measurement of social benefits, and possible trade-offs between financial and social returns continue to prevent many institutional investors from pursuing either ETIs or from choosing money managers who pursue social investment strategies.

The Jessie Smith Noyes Foundation

The Jessie Smith Noyes Foundation, with assets of approximately $60 million and grant allocations of about $3.5 million per year, has two goals:
- Preventing irreversible damage to the natural systems upon which all life depends.
- Strengthening individuals and institutions committed to protecting natural systems and ensuring a sustainable society.

Involved with social investing since the 1980s, during the last two years the Foundation has redefined its investment policy as part of a process of redefining "fiduciary responsibility" for itself.

Our premises may be summarized informally as follows:
- What good are good returns if you cannot drink the water or breathe the air?
- Fiduciary responsibility must be subsumed by institutional or corporate responsibility, not the other way around.

We believe that it is our responsibility to view our assets, as well as our income, as tools for social change. Repercussions with respect to the behavior of the companies in which we invest are, however indirectly, our responsibility. The full scope of this responsibility can be summarized in a simple question: How does the commercial activity that our investments finance affect stakeholders or damage the environment, now and in coming years?

Stakeholders include employees, customers, suppliers, and communities in which companies do business. Recognized, here, is our fiduciary responsibility to understand the use of our assets not only in terms of the financial needs of our beneficiaries (in this case, grantees), but also in terms of impact on the environment, the economy, and democracy as a whole.

Such an approach stands in contrast to that of the foundation sector as a whole. Paradoxically, the bifurcation between profit-maximizing and social purpose is nowhere more pronounced than within foundations, where the iron curtain between endowment management and the grant-making program is virtually inviolable in the name of "making as much as possible so we will have more to give away." Program officers focus on their obligations to foundations' primary constituency, grantees. Treasurers, finance committees and money managers focus on what they know best. For the most part, the two sides of the house share neither training, temperament, nor professional goals, and their interaction is minimal.

"Compared to other components of foundation philanthropy, endowment has little natural appeal," suggests one observer. "It projects none of the excitement of bold program initiatives, diversity among trustees or strategic, proactive grantmaking."[6] Irene Diamond of the Diamond Foundation takes the case one step further. "Most foundations spend very little of their money. They're in the investment business." Seeing the choice between either "profit-maximizing" or "giving it all away," the Diamond Foundation has chosen the latter course, proceeding on a pace of giving that will spend the foundation out of existence in a few years.[7]

In response to a similar recognition of the "dissonance" between philanthropic initiatives and investment management, the Jessie Smith Noyes Foundation has chosen a different course. Our investment policy appears in Figure 2. We have chosen to align our asset management with our mission.

What has this meant in practical terms? First, we have placed all of our public equities with three managers – US Trust, Franklin Research, and Winslow Management, all in Boston – who evaluate social and environmental impact along with financial performance and who are willing to work with us interactively as we refine our strategies and screens. We are also working similarly with our fixed-income portfolio manager, Bear Stearns. Second, we have allocated five percent of our assets to direct venture capital investments in private companies whose business is consistent with our mission. By the end of 1994, we will have invested roughly $1,000,000 in several early-stage companies, including an energy services company, a developer and marketer of enzyme-based cleaning products, and a manufacturer of leak detection systems for underground storage tanks.

Third, we are exploring the efficacy of communicating our concerns directly to management of companies whose stock we hold. For example, as a sizable supporter of sustainable agriculture with our

---

[6] Scooler, Dean. "Endowments: Indispensable Storehouse for the Future." *Foundation News and Commentary,* May/June, 1994, pp. 30–32.
[7] "One Foundation's Aim: Spend Till the End," *New York Times,* March 14, 1994, p. A1.

FIGURE 2

The Jessie Smith Noyes Foundation Investment Policy

Statement of Responsibility

We begin the endowment management process recognizing that our responsibility does not end with maximizing return and minimizing risk. We recognize that economic growth can come at considerable cost to community and environment. We believe that efforts to mitigate environmental degradation, address issues of social justice and promote community development will be successful to the extent that these concerns are brought from the margins to the center of business and investment decisionmaking.

We recognize that addressing such concerns while pursuing financial objectives is an imperfect process. However, we believe that the development of healthier corporate cultures, and through them a healthier, sustainable economy, depends upon the recognition of these concerns by management, directors, employees and investors. Within foundations, this means reducing the dissonance between charitable mission and endowment management.

We believe that in light of the social, environmental and economic challenges of our time, fiduciary responsibility in the coming decades will dictate the integration of prudent financial management practices with principles of environmental stewardship and corporate citizenship. Foundations have a particular role to play in this process, by coming to understand their mission not only in terms of the uses of income to fund programs, but also in terms of the ends toward which endowment assets are managed.

Investment Goals and Guidelines

The Jessie Smith Noyes Foundation seeks to preserve its real purchasing power over time through a diversified portfolio of stocks, bonds, and alternative investments, utilizing to the extent possible investment managers who achieve competitive financial returns through the application of social and environmental screens. In concert with the Foundation's mission to preserve the environment, promote sustainable community development, and support innovative individuals and organizations, we seek to invest our endowment assets in companies that:

• provide commercial solutions to major social and environmental problems; and/or
• build corporate culture around concerns for environmental impact, equity, and sustainable community development.

The *environmental impact* of a business is tied to the throughput of materials as well as to the long-term value of the goods or services it produces. *Equity* within a corporation derives from participatory management, employee ownership, salary structures, workforce diversity, employee benefit programs, or other demonstrated commitments to the well-being of all individuals involved in an enterprise. A corporation can promote *sustainable community develop-*

ment through local job creation for the economically disadvantaged, corporate giving to and active involvement with community organizations, or other initiatives that provide net benefits to the local economy.

In evaluating the environmental impact of a company, we look for:

- stated environmental policies;
- record of regulatory compliance;
- on-going audit program that goes beyond regulatory requirements;
- record of waste and toxic emission reduction, including commitment to reuse and recycling;
- R&D funding for new processes and materials that minimize environmental impact.

We will not invest in companies that:

- produce and/or utilize nuclear power (including those that mine uranium ore or develop or maintain nuclear reactors);
- produce synthetic pesticides, herbicides, or other agricultural chemicals;
- engage in the manufacture, processing, or marketing of food in a manner inconsistent with sustainable agriculture;
- derive more than five percent of their revenue from the manufacture and sale of tobacco products.

In industries that do not meet our screens, companies that have signed the CERES Principles or demonstrated particular leadership within their industry with respect to social responsibility and environmental impact may be considered on a case by case basis.

---

philanthropic dollars, we are cautious about agribusiness companies even when they pass the general social screens of our money managers. In the case of a large food distributor, we have initiated correspondence to further probe corporate positions with regard to farming practices of suppliers, corporate involvement at the community level, and a number of other concerns. We are also currently working with a number of our sustainable agriculture grantees to identify areas of strategic opportunity, in order to effectively target investment initiatives in this area. We became engaged with management of another portfolio company, Intel, when we discovered that one of our grantees, the Southwest Organizing Project (SWOP), was challenging the company.

Intel, SWOP, and the Process of Engagement

The Southwest Organizing Project is a respected grassroots group based in Albuquerque that focuses on issues of economic and environmental justice and voter registration in New Mexico. In response to what they perceived as a giveaway by the state of New Mexico to

Intel, as part of the company's expansion into the state of its micro-chip production, SWOP prepared an in-depth report.[8] Issues ad-dressed included state permits for excessive air pollution and water use in the desert, and financial inducements in the form of loans and tax breaks amounting to more than $250,000 per job promised by Intel. We decided, in conjunction with SWOP, that it would be useful for the Foundation to attend Intel's 1994 annual shareholders' meet-ing in Albuquerque and ask that the company respond to the issues SWOP had raised in its report.

At the meeting, in response to our request, Intel management stated that it was the company's policy to deal with responsible elected officials, rather than with "vocal minorities." They avoided our request for a written reply.

Subsequently, one of our money managers, Winslow Management, became involved, ultimately visiting SWOP and Intel, in turn, and reporting the situation in its newsletter. Another of our managers, Franklin Research, also researched the situation, publicizing it in their newsletter. A number of articles appeared in newspapers and financial publications calling attention to the effort, which got re-sponses from other investors, who also contacted Intel. In November 1994, a shareholder resolution was initiated by the Noyes Founda-tion, in cooperation with ICCR and others, addressing issues of cor-porate accountability and transparency to the community.

It now appears that a meeting between Intel and SWOP may occur. Whatever the outcome, we will be assessing on an ongoing basis the efficacy of this type of shareholder involvement by the Foundation.

Corporate Culture and Sustainability

Our involvement with SWOP and Intel vividly underscores the challenges and opportunities created when one takes an alternative approach to what has traditionally been perceived as a dichotomy between asset management and social purpose. In such alternatives may lie powerful tools for addressing the social and environmental challenges of our time.

Given the magnitude of these challenges, not only must the left hand know what the right hand is doing, but new strategies must be developed and implemented to effectively bring all means at our dis-

---

[8] South West Organizing Project, *Intel Inside New Mexico,* Albuquerque, May 1994.

posal to bear, not just to enhance our well-being, but, quite possibly, to ensure our survival. Assets must be deployed strategically towards solving large and small problems, not only because problems sometimes translate into new markets, but also because philanthropy and the public sector cannot, by themselves, do what has to be done.

The benefits of growth in assets are illusory to the extent that they compromise or destroy the environment, which is the basis of all life and all production. Or, as Wendell Berry observes, "An economy that sees the life of a community or a place as expendable, and reckons its value only in terms of money, is not acceptable because it is not realistic."[9]

Incorporating what we have come to know about the realities of industrial pollution and the potential for large scale, irreversible damage to natural systems, fiduciaries in the late twentieth century must reckon with the new realities of money management. They must develop a new realism. What was prudent at the inception of the industrial revolution and through various stages of ensuing economic growth is no longer prudent at the threshold of a ten-billion-person globe with a hole in its ozone layer.

Through their investment programs, financial institutions can send critical signals to corporate management and capital markets, encouraging or discouraging integration of concerns about social and environmental impact into decision-making and playing a fundamental role in the process of steering business toward or away from sustainability. By viewing financial assets as resources that can be employed in the service of our goals, rather than as pools of passive income-generating securities, financial institutions can begin the long process of "healing" the bifurcation between social purpose and making money, and so help reinvent corporate cultures, both their own and those of the companies in which they are investing.

Through a new, more realistic understanding of prudence and fiduciary responsibility, institutional investors can nurture a new generation of healthier, more humane, more sustainable companies and, through them, an environment within which healthier communities and a more humane, more sustainable economy can emerge.

---

[9] Berry, Wendell. *What Are People For?* San Francisco: North Point Press, 1990, p. 113.

Part Three:
Implementation

10

Industrial Clusters of the Twenty-first Century

Gunter Pauli

Throughout this book we have discussed the challenge for business to survive and flourish at a time when the industrialized world is going through a dramatic change of paradigms, from a mechanistic to an ecological world view, from a value system emphasizing expansion, competition, and domination to one guided by conservation, cooperation, and partnership.

A paradigm is a constellation of concepts, perceptions, values, and practices shared by a community and embodied in its social institutions. In our modern era, technology has become one of the most important embodiments of the mechanistic paradigm. Throughout the industrialized world, individuals and institutions have become mesmerized by the wonders of modern technology and have come to believe that every problem has a technological solution. Whether the nature of the problem is political, psychological, or economic, the first reaction, almost automatically, is to deal with it by applying or developing some new technology.

We do not share this belief, although we see technology as an important part of the move toward sustainability, and therefore we have left the discussion of new technologies to the last section of this book. Before we enter into the dialogue on new technologies, we should perhaps clarify the general meaning and purpose of technology.

Contrary to widespread belief, technology is never value-free, because it is defined as a means to a certain end. Good technology, by definition, is a proper means to a carefully considered end, and value judgments will be involved both in the selection of the end and in the decision of what constitutes proper means. In any society the technologies used will therefore embody the predominant paradigm.

Even a cursory look at our "high technologies" – military, medical, agricultural, or any other – shows clearly that they embody the mechanistic paradigm and associated value system. They are fragmented rather than integrative, designed for manipulation and control rather than cooperation and partnership, and suitable for centralized management rather than regional application by individuals and small groups. As a result, these technologies have become profoundly anti-ecological, antisocial, unhealthy, and inhuman.

Moreover, technology in our era has become autonomous and totalitarian, redefining our basic concepts, eliminating alternative worldviews, and subjugating all forms of cultural expression. In today's "high-tech" world, progress is no longer understood as the improvement of human well-being but is glibly identified with technological innovation.

Thus the first step in developing technologies that are ecologically sustainable must be to transform the very nature of technology from a totalitarian "megatechnology" to a tool, the use of which is restricted by cultural norms. This means that in any discussion of new technologies much thought should be given to their goals and purposes, as well as to whether a particular technology is the most appropriate means to the intended end.

When these considerations are applied to the task of steering business toward sustainability, it becomes clear that the technologies most appropriate for this purpose will embody the paradigm of deep ecology. In other words, they will reflect the wisdom of nature and incorporate the principles of ecology in their design.

One of the most outstanding principles of ecology is the cyclical nature of ecological processes. As Fritjof Capra pointed out in Chapter 1, the present clash between business and nature, between economics and ecology, is mainly due to the fact that nature is cyclical whereas our industrial systems are linear. In order to achieve ecological sustainability we must therefore fundamentally redesign our businesses and our economy so that they imitate the cyclical patterns observed in nature. Just as the wastes from one species are food for other species in an ecosystem, so one industry's waste must become another industry's resource in a sustainable business world.

This issue is taken up by Gunter Pauli in the present chapter. Pauli is a businessman who has established numerous companies, has busi-

ness contacts in Europe, Asia, Africa, and the Americas, and has traveled widely in all those parts of the world. His talent for spotting emerging trends, his solid business background, and his penchant for radical ecological solutions have allowed him to piece together a picture of emerging industrial clusters, patterned after natural ecological cycles, which is visionary and yet thoroughly pragmatic.

What do perfumes, food stabilizers, forestry, and beer brewing have in common? At first sight, little or nothing at all. What do paper and pulp, construction materials, packaging and printing ink have to do with each other? Nothing whatsoever, would one say. What does sugar share with detergents, water softeners and plastics? Absolutely nothing, one would argue at first sight. But, if you start analyzing the potential synergies between these sectors when their strategies and innovations are based on sustainable economic development, we are looking at the new clusters of industry for the 21st century.

Zero Defects, Zero Inventory, Zero Emissions

Over the next decade, industry will have to re-engineer manufacturing and convert itself into a zero-emissions production system. After the quest for zero defects and zero inventory, zero emissions will become a standard objective for production engineers. This process of eliminating all forms of waste is nothing more than a persistent drive to cut costs. It will also give rise to an industrial integration quite distinct from the vertical integration traditionally sought after by industrial groupings. Sectors which seem to have little in common will become closely linked. Industrial policy makers will have to plan for a new form of industrial cooperation when targeting new investments.

Today, zero emissions production is considered impossible, or at least too expensive to be feasible under market conditions. But, though industry twenty years ago did not accept that it had to manufacture with perfect quality, i.e., zero defects, today it is clear to all actors in the market that unless one produces perfect quality, one cannot compete. Quality was first considered an extra cost, then it became profitable through lowered servicing costs, and gradually perfect quality became a competitive tool. Today, perfect quality is considered a precondition to market entry. Similarly, today few believe that zero emissions is feasible, but in twenty years it will be the standard.

147

Companies that wish to maintain their position in the market, build up their competitive edge, and maintain a solid image with their stakeholders (clients, shareholders, local community) have embarked on programs to reduce waste. The drive towards energy efficiency certainly was the first necessary step, but environmental problems, widely highlighted in the international media, have motivated companies to go beyond a mere look at energy efficiency, sewage, and air pollution.

Front-end Solutions Versus End-of-the-Pipe Solutions

The internalization of many real costs of production, which now have to be borne by the polluter, has already made clear to many industrialists that it is better to reduce the cost of waste at the front end, than to have to cope with ever changing and complex environmental regulations and increasing burden of environmental taxes affecting the waste discharged "at the end of the pipe." But, while all this is to be applauded, a bolder step is needed to leapfrog in competitiveness. Industry must be willing to put its present selection of raw materials under scrutiny, rethink the manufacturing and distribution process, and be ready to engage in a search for zero emissions manufacturing.

Today industry depends heavily on raw materials which are not sustainable. We have evolved in a system where we know that several of the key input factors will not be available any more in twenty or thirty years. With the massive demand of six billion consumers today, and probably ten billion by the time the earth runs out of petroleum, there is a need to identify alternatives early on. The Club of Rome called for this long ago in the widely debated *Limits to Growth* report (1974).

The good news is that there are numerous opportunities to pursue alternatives, but unfortunately, these are not pursued with the vigor needed to convert our industries and consumption patterns to sustainable ones. However, the search for new materials offers a unique chance to re-engineer these innovations along sustainability lines.

Economies of Scale

The manufacturing process is based on ever-increasing economies of scale. The search for ever lower marginal costs has resulted after forty years in a highly complex, capital-intensive, centralized, and inflexible production system which is very dependent on cheap forms of transportation. The break-even point of factories has increased by a factor of 50 to 100 over the past forty years. The re-engineering of industry which we are witnessing today includes even a further – and perhaps last – push towards concentration of production, which implies closing factories and laying off employees. This is not a sustainable form of industrial development.

Industry will have to redesign operations around a new type of economy of scale, probably tailored after the Coca-Cola approach, a prime example of sustainable industrial development designed with competitiveness in mind, not driven by the moral need to save mother earth.

Coca-Cola, without intending it, is a surprisingly good example of how sustainable development can be combined with highly decentralized production and a great capability to adapt to changing local market conditions.

High Economies of Scale *The Procter & Gamble Approach*	Appropriate Economies of Scale *The Coca-Cola Approach*
high capital intensive	low capital intensive
high break-even point	low break-even point
high risk	low risk
slow response to change	immediate response to change
complex to operate	simple to operate
centralized controls	decentralized decision making
difficult environmental stewardship	sustainable production method
limited local partnership	many local partnerships
reducing employment	increasing employment
closing factories in the 90s	opening factories in the 90s
RESULT: losing market share	*strengthening market share*

The Coca-Cola bottling concept has not only evolved over a century into a corporate structure which is an example for the future, but it has rendered the company a clear leader in its business. Coca-Cola has strengthened its market position and continues to expand along the same line whereas another prime example in the fast-moving consumer goods market, Procter & Gamble, is closing 30 factories over the next four years and plans to lay off more than 10,000 employees in an effort to stem the loss of market share.

If manufacturing is based on a decentralized concept with lower levels of economies of scale, then it will be better equipped for global competition. It represents lower levels of capital investment, easier adaptation to changes in demand, and greater involvement of local capital. The lower level of economies of scale will facilitate environmental stewardship. After all, it is easier to take care of waste in a small operation than in a 10,000 employees, billion dollar turnover type of operation.

Will Japan Embrace the ZERO Concept?

Japanese industry, recognized for having forced the rest of the world to pay attention to the need for higher productivity, perfect quality, and just-in-time delivery of parts, seems ready to embrace this zero-emissions concept. After all, any form of waste is a sign of inefficiency. The economic grail of "minimum input – maximum output" will only be attained when there is "total throughput." There is room for dramatic improvement as long as *any* input factors are discarded.

Our economic system cannot be considered efficient, or ultimately competitive, if it generates waste. The concept of "from cradle to grave" actually accepts waste as a normal part of the process. Thus we embark on broad programs to recycle. This is the strategy applied today. There is a need to integrate a new concept, "from cradle to cradle."[1] This is the strategy of tomorrow. All forms of waste must become the inputs and raw materials for another production cycle. After all, this is how nature disposes of its wastes, and this is the only way that we can secure a long term sustainable industrial process.

The New Clusters

These developments and trends point to the emergence of new clusters of industry. A few concrete examples will clarify the argument. Take the case of de-inking and recycling of paper. No one will argue against the fact that the recycling of paper will become a growing industrial activity in the years ahead. Countries which have no paper and pulp industry of their own but are great consumers of paper will be driven particularly strongly towards the establishment of de-inking operations. Japan, Taiwan, Hong Kong, Singapore, and in the future China are most affected.

---

[1] This concept was developed by Dr. Michael Braungart, founder and president of the Environmental Protection Encouragement Agency in Hamburg, Germany.

Recycling of Ink and Paper

De-inking today is a polluting, inefficient, and expensive process. Present de-inking technologies do not succeed in removing more than 65–70% of the ink particles from the wood fibers. That is the reason why recycled paper has a gray look. The waste created in the process of recycling is a toxic, useless mixture of ink, short fibers, and chemicals. It requires both primary and secondary treatment, and thus represents high capital investments. As a result of the inefficiencies of the system, recycled paper is more expensive and is of lower quality than new paper made from freshly cut trees, even when the raw material, used paper, is obtained free of charge.

Traditional Recycling Thinking Recycle paper	Zero Emissions Thinking Recycle ink and paper

inefficient: only 65% de-inking
highly polluting: toxic sludge
highly capital intensive
    due to water treatment
    systems and bleaching
expensive to the consumer
replacing one problem with
    another problem
no net economic effect
	efficient: 100% recycling of ink
	zero emissions: 100% re-use
	lower capital needs
	
	price competitive
	total problem solving
	
	creation of new industries

MISSING LINK: technology to separate ink from fiber	

If a new technology were to be developed that permits the perfect and clean non-toxic separation of ink particles from the wood fibers, then we would see at once the emergence of several new industrial activities. A world of science and technology that is capable of cloning human genes and putting men on the moon should have the ingenuity to design a process that detaches ink from paper in an efficient way.

Such de-inking would offer three outputs: (1) ink which can be re-used for printing, which actually means the recycling of ink; there is also an option to use this ink for pencils too often still based on lead, (2) long fibers completely void of residue ink and thus needing no further bleaching, ready to be remade into paper, and (3) a sludge of short fibers and residues from the process such as coating chemicals

151

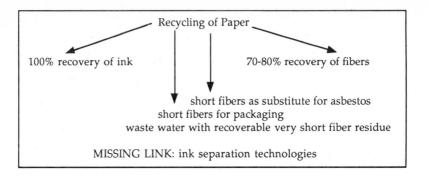

and clay. This sludge has numerous potential applications. It can be used in a dried pulpy form as a noise absorber, filling air in the inner walls separating two rooms. It is a construction material. As these dried fibers, mixed with the coating chemicals, are bacteria-resistant and of a quality approaching asbestos, other light-weight construction materials can be made from it. Ceiling tiles are a simple application.

The short fibers and the residue could also be transformed into packaging material which is shock absorbent and could replace styro-foam "peanuts." It could also be turned into egg packaging. In any case, the packaging industry would have an interest in it. This actually implies that the partial recycling of paper and the 100% recycling of ink leads to a cluster of four industries: paper, ink, construction materials, and packaging materials.

Cities, states and national governments pass laws requiring the use of recycled paper. But the policy makers have only a limited vision of the industries that it could actually create. Little if any attention is reserved for the technological breakthroughs that are needed to make the recycling economical and environmentally benign. Local governments, consumers and industry have embarked on often ambitious paper recycling programs. But, consider the positive impact on job creation, inner city development, and pollution prevention schemes that these initiatives and efforts will have once the technological breakthrough has been achieved.

Forestry, Perfumes, and Preservatives

A few additional examples will clarify the point of the new clusters and offer a preview of some of the most important ones. Take forestry, where extractive practices are under heavy legal and political pressure. The bitterness of the struggle has obscured great opportunities that are waiting to be tapped.

Felled trees are normally stripped of the green mass and branches at the place of logging. Several types of pine trees (not all) produce excellent perfume, leaf proteins, stabilizers (preservatives) for food processing, and a series of color pigments. The distillation process required to obtain these products is highly energy intensive. Small-scale on-site distillation units can utilize small wood debris for the needed heat energy. It is possible to produce, out of one ton of green mass, some 1-2 gallons of essential oils and stabilizers of varied quality, some of which are highly priced and command a price of US$ 100 a gallon.

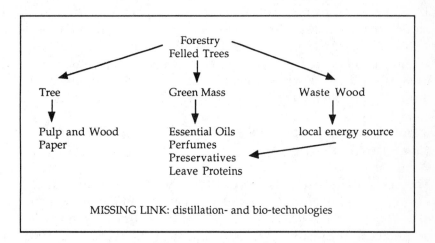

The world market for synthetic perfumes is large and very profitable. But many synthetic perfumes are under scrutiny because these aromatic molecular structures are highly allergenic and are difficult to degrade. Natural perfumes are not significantly allergenic and bio-degrade easily. In addition, demand for natural perfumes due to the rise in consumers' interest in aromatherapy is increasing rapidly. This leads to high prices for quality products. The mark-up for imported essential oils in Japan reached the incredible 100 mark, a proof of the lack of supply.

The same goes for the preservatives. Contemporary food processing is impossible without advanced forms of preservation. The use of chemical preservatives is under pressure for health and environmental reasons and numerous alternative forms of preservation are being sought. Pine trees have a remarkable ability to survive temperature extremes. Biologists know that several of their components are of great value, but the present abundant and cheap availability of synthetic materials has not opened the market for the natural alternative. This will change. An extraction method will offer the chance to isolate these natural substitutes for which over time there will be a strong demand. Additional research is necessary.

The world's forestry companies, logging approximately 45 million hectares annually, are certainly the most important potential producers of preservatives and essential oils. They have the raw material and the energy source. If a decentralized distillation system is put in place, i.e. the smallest possible economy of scale, this will not only be a major new business, it will also be a source of jobs which will need the expertise which can be drawn from the loggers and the foresters who know best the key resource for both industries. And, from a revenue point of view, the additional income earned by making use of what is considered waste today, could very well complement the turnover generated by the traditional mainstream businesses.

Sugar, Cleansing Materials, Water Softeners and Compostable Plastics

The sugar industry offers another exciting new cluster. Sugar is a world commodity, produced on all continents. But the present change in consumer preferences for low-calorie synthetic sweeteners has led to a massive over-supply on the world sugar markets. The price for this natural commodity has dropped below production cost. Numerous developing countries are suffering from a drop in foreign-exchange revenues. Whereas today sugar is mainly associated with food and, in Brazil, Hawaii, and other places with gasohol production or the generation of electricity by the burning of sugar-cane stalks, a whole variety of new industries are likely to emerge.

First of all, detergents. Several derivatives of sugar are excellent cleaners. APG (alkyl polyglucose) is perhaps the most attractive modern-day cleaning agent. Based on sugar, it is used in a limited form for cosmetics as a skin and hair cleanser and in pharmaceutical applications to speed up the absorption of active ingredients into the bloodstream. APGs could quickly become an excellent substitute for the synthetic detergents which use a non-renewable source (petroleum) or a product from highly polluting monocultures (coconut plantations). The sugar-based APG is a hundred times easier to degrade and is as effective.

Sugar also has a great potential for the making of plastics. At a time when chlorine-based plastics, such as polyvinyl chloride (PVC) are under pressure, alternatives can be drawn from sugar. One option foresees the distillation of ethylene from sugar; it is then polymerized into polyethylene, a common form of plastic. A second option is to ferment sugar into plastics by using yeasts which feed on the sugar and convert up to 75% of their weight into a plastic-like base material.

There are more applications for sugar such as the use of its derivatives as a substitute for phosphates, a raw material banned in many countries for adverse effects on the environment. CITREX is an excellent water softener with wide application opportunities in any country with hard-water conditions. These are just some of the first most obvious applications.

It is impossible for the sugar farmers who have accumulated a vast experience in raising the crop, and have billions of capital investments in farming equipment, to convert this crop into a new type of commodity. The option is either to find a new crop and income for several years while writing off their investments, or to find new applications for the sugar. The second option is the most appropriate, and will bring industry closer together with agriculture to form a formidable new alliance.

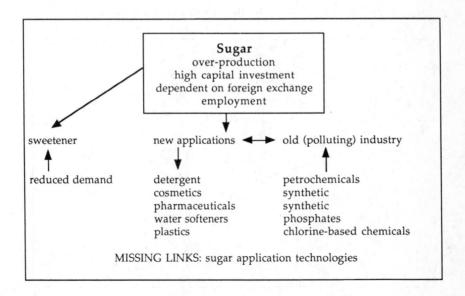

MISSING LINKS: sugar application technologies

Beer, Salmon, and Cattle

The brewing of beer creates numerous environmental headaches. The process is far from zero-emissions but could be converted into a perfectly sustainable industry. One of its most polluting activities is the cleansing of the beer-brewing installations. Harsh chemicals are needed to meet strict health standards. As a result, the system needs to be cleaned twice, once with chemicals and again with water to rinse out the chemicals.

If sugar based cleaners are used, the waste water could be fed to fish farms. As we know, eating sugar makes you fat. Why not combine the two, cleaning the system and feeding the fish? In addition, the solid waste from the breweries is rich in protein. This residue has always been used to feed cattle, until the feedlot operations became so massive that the handling of the waste stream became highly polluting. Smaller breweries still have excellent opportunities to provide input to both cattle and fish farmers, a cluster of agro-industry never looked at as being complementary.

The cleansing of returned bottles of beer or milk could be reintegrated along the same lines, securing the elimination of plastic bottles, a major source of municipal solid waste. Whether we talk about milk, juices, beer, or sodas, we actually have a wide variety of product residues which could be removed with natural ingredients. The resulting mixture is excellent for fish farming. The recycling of glass bottles on a local scale becomes most attractive, not just from an environmental point of view, but even more from a food-production perspective.

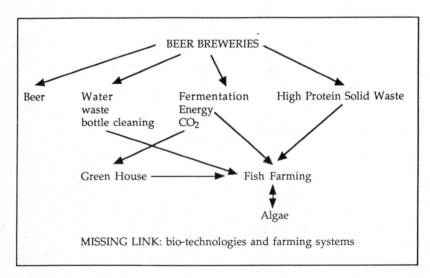

MISSING LINK: bio-technologies and farming systems

In a whole continent such as Africa, with breweries as every nation's pride, there is no one considering the possible integration of fish farming, breweries, and sugar industries. At a time when the world's wild fish catch has clearly reached absolute limits, the drive towards fish farming will intensify. The question is how to secure food for the fish. Using waste from the cleansing process is a research program that has started in China in cooperation with scientists from around the world.

More to Come

New clusters will shape industrial policies and corporate strategies of the 21st century. Those industrialists who see this will be able to undertake partnerships, R&D programs, acquisitions, and new start-ups, which may not be understood by their competitors or shareholders, but which will position them for the 21st century's competition.

All forms of waste will have to be integrated into the mechanism. Waste from one industry, in whatever form, must become an input factor for another business. Companies will decide to locate next to each other because they need each others' wastes. Cities and counties will target specific investments because they realize that attracting one is likely to attract another one, while solving a pressing environmental problem at the same time.

Improving the efficiency of industry, securing investments, implementing inner-city development, and enhancing sustainable social and economic development for the first time can go hand in hand. The time has come to put it into practice. Those who do so will go down in history books as the visionaries of the 21st century. Those who don't will have lost jobs and competitiveness.

Rethinking Industrial Policies

Government at local and regional levels around the world is under great pressure to create new jobs. The high level of unemployment on one hand and the dramatic numbers of young graduates seeking jobs puts a tremendous pressure on the policy makers. They have to find ways to stimulate economic activity.

The emergence of the new industrial clusters described here will offer cities, regions, and countries which see this opportunity an edge in mobilizing investments. The infrastructural needs can be tailored to the new industrial clusters and campaigns to attract specific companies can be oriented towards this new vision. It will render the industrial partners more competitive and the overall scheme less costly.

Cutting Government Costs

This "cradle to cradle" concept represents new dynamics in the market. It will change the face of industry. The first one to benefit is the government (industrial policy makers and city authorities) and thus the tax payer. Indeed, if industry over the next two decades adopts zero emissions as a standard, then we will observe one of the biggest cuts in government budgets: i.e., the elimination of the need to invest in expensive infrastructure for handling the solid and other wastes produced by ordinary industries.

Let us face the facts. An industrial park requires today a massive up-front investment from local and national governments. The construction of the industrial sewage system, high-volume and high-pressure fresh water supply, high-voltage electricity, stabilized roads, and the like are multi-million dollar investments made decades in advance. Without these investments, no industry would even consider establishing an operation.

But, consider the following possibility: industry reduces water consumption by a factor of ten, has no need for an industrial sewage system because it reuses all waste water itself, energy efficiency is improved by a factor of five, and manufacturing is decentralized instead of highly centralized so that there is no need for high voltage. This changes the face of the industrial parks' infrastructural outlay and the budget needed to prepare for the investments. It has been estimated by the author that as much as 80% of the typical investment needed to prepare an area as an industrial park can be eliminated.

Revitalizing the Inner Cities

There is a second impact of this evolution. Thanks to (1) the highly flexible and local-market-oriented economies of scale and (2) the zero emissions standard, industry can reestablish its operations back in the city centers. After all, industry was driven out of downtowns because it needed cheap land to build very large single-story plants and was a nuisance to the citizens due to its air, water and noise pollution. But under the new conditions, there is a chance to put life back into the inner cities which are often struggling to get their poverty-ridden and crime-prone areas back on their feet.

The Case of China

To conclude let us reflect on what "zero emissions" represents for an industrializing nation such as China.[2]

Since 1950, world production of paper has expanded sixfold, and the industry currently has a world trade value of about US$50 billion. Today, China already counts among the four largest paper producers, but the consumption per capita is twenty times lower than the US and Japan. The United States, Japan, Canada, and China together account for over half of the world total production. Sixty percent of Chinese paper is manufactured with non-wood pulp, and many waste fibers are being considered for paper-making.

Asia imported almost 6.5 million tons of wastepaper in 1992. Taiwan is the world's largest net importer, South Korea was the second, followed by China and Indonesia. These data indicate the acute situation in Asia and the need to address recycling in a fundamental way. Rising literacy rates will further contribute to the increase in paper use. The introduction of fast copiers, printers, and word processing programs make it possible to reproduce effortless and rapidly. Nearly none of this office automation is widely available in China.

The zero-emissions research initiative is a not just an opportunity for Japanese, European, and North American paper and pulp industries to change the face of industry, it is a matter of necessity in view of the dramatic increase of demand expected and the absolute need to stem the adverse side effects of present de-inking methods.

If China were to consume as much paper per capita as the Japanese and the Americans, it would be absolutely mandatory that all paper be recycled on the basis of a zero-emissions concept. If not, the world would be confronted with a dramatic rise in pulp prices. If recycling through de-inking remains based on the current flotation method, a huge sludge of water, ink, chemicals, and short fibers will threaten not only the Chinese rivers, but the Japan Sea as well.

The same logic applies to aquaculture and beer brewing. With the global fish catch declining and with population continuing to expand, the per capita catch is falling fast. The effects of overfishing, pollution, and coastal habitat destruction increase the need to supplement the shortage of supply with fish farming. China dominates world fish farming, producing almost half of the world total. In China, produc-

---

[2] Data on paper industry and fish farming are derived from *Vital Signs 1994*, published by the Worldwatch Institute Inc., 1776 Massachusetts Ave., NW, Washington DC 20036.

tion from fish farms is as large as the wild catch. Asia produces 80% of the farmed seafood worldwide.

Aquaculture has an advantage over its competitors – pork, chicken, and beef – because fish farming is more efficient. Growing a kilogram of beef in a feedlot takes 7 kilograms of feed. A kilogram of pork requires 4 kilograms of feed. And although chicken is the most efficient of the land-raised meats, it still takes an estimated 2.2 kilograms of feed to yield a kilogram of chicken. Fish, in contrast, need 2 kilograms or less of feed. Suspended in the water, fish do not have to expend many calories to move about, and since they are cold-blooded, they do not burn calories to heat their bodies.

Aquaculture can grow, but if it continues to increase at present rates in China, it will require roughly 1 million additional tons of grain every year. That could become too high a cost to pay. At a time when the world carryover stocks of grains (the amount of grain in the bins when the new harvest begins) are projected to drop from 351 million tons in 1993 to 290 million tons in 1994, innovative approaches are needed.

If the Chinese are to embark on investment in breweries, it would be a loss of energy and opportunities unless this policy foresees the establishment of fish farms next to the breweries. While this is a novelty for industrial planners, it will be a necessity. As world grain-land production has only risen one percent between 1984 and 1993, well below population growth, a fundamental rethinking is necessary to safeguard future supply.

And then there are plastics. There is no question about the fact that the Chinese will quickly exhaust all petrochemical resources if they were to package their vegetables and fruits as the Japanese do. Did anyone ever dare to calculate how many millions of tons of additional waste plastics this will add to the garbage stream? Unless these plastics are designed to be compostable, the world will witness an explosion in demand for petrochemicals and an uncontrollable mountain of waste.

The only way that we can imagine the overall improvement of standards of living for the 1.4 billion Chinese is if all forms of waste are eliminated and transformed into input factors for another industrial process, not as a source of energy, but as a value added. These two cases of aquaculture and paper recycling offer interesting alternatives which must be researched systematically alongside numerous additional opportunities.

The Role of the United Nations University

This is why the United Nations University (UNU) is embarking on a major research program dedicated to zero emissions. ZERI, the Zero Emissions Research Initiative, aims to bring the best researchers in a multi-disciplinary manner together with the most important industrial policy makers and industry representatives. The objective is to have the first tangible results within five years.

The United Nations University was established in 1973 after a proposal from Secretary General U Thant. The UNU is an international community of scholars engaged in research, post-graduate training, and the dissemination of knowledge through a center located in Tokyo and a network of research and training centers located in the developed and developing countries. From its headquarters in Japan it promotes long-term, global, and multi-disciplinary research. The Zero Emission Research Initiative is the first attempt to bring industry, industrial policy makers, and researchers together under the UN umbrella.

Conclusion

The present market system is unquestionably more economically efficient than a centralized planning system. But our market system cannot be considered the best possible solution. Its deficiencies must be addressed. The economic axiom of minimum input and maximum output naturally leads to the goal of total throughput with no waste – the highest level of efficiency that can be achieved. While this goal is logical, it will require a massive effort from scientists to invent the new technologies needed, from business to identify the synergies required, from entrepreneurs to capitalize on the new opportunities traditional management neglects, and from the government to adopt an industrial policy framework.

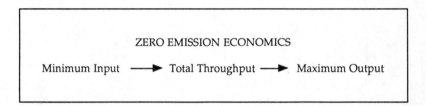

ZERO EMISSION ECONOMICS

Minimum Input ⟶ Total Throughput ⟶ Maximum Output

The countries which will envision these new clusters first and stimulate an environment conducive to this change will be the new tigers of the 21st century. The countries that hang on to the old system will be the dinosaurs. The difference will be made by the men and women who see this today and who will make it happen tomorrow.

11

Living Machines

John Todd and Nancy Jack Todd

This chapter continues our exploration of technologies that incorporate the ecological wisdom of nature. It introduces our readers to what we consider today's most advanced and most revolutionary technologies of this kind. The authors have been on the forefront of these revolutionary developments for the past twenty-five years. John Todd, visionary biologist and ecological designer, is the founder of the now-legendary New Alchemy Institute and the Center of Restoration of Waters at Ocean Arks International in Massachusetts, where he has pioneered "living technologies," and in particular the "living machines" described in the following pages.

Nancy Jack Todd has been active in the environmental movement for over two decades. As cofounder of the New Alchemy Institute, editor of its journals, vice president of Ocean Arks, and editor of their publication, Annals of Earth, *she has been the primary force behind communicating their results to a worldwide readership. Both authors have published numerous articles and several books on ecological design, including most recently the jointly authored volume,* From Eco-Cities to Living Machines: Principles of Ecological Design *(1994).*

This chapter is an inspiring introduction to a novel and wonderful branch of ecological design. As the authors explain, a living machine is a contained ecosystem comprising hundreds, even thousands, of species of carefully selected organisms. It is a machine, because it has been designed and built to perform specific tasks. At the same time, however, it is fundamentally different from conventional machines and even from standard biotechnologies.

The design of these new, human-created ecosystems not only in-

corporates all the principles of ecology, but also uses the inherent intelligence of the ecological community contained in the structure. Like natural ecosystems, living machines are capable of repairing themselves, replacing their components as they wear out, and of responding creatively to change by "evolutionary" self-design.

Living machines have been designed and built to produce food, heat and cool buildings, treat wastes, and purify the air. Most astonishingly, they can perform all of these functions simultaneously. Prototypes of these miracles of ecological design are now being installed throughout the United States, and in Canada, the United Kingdom, and Australia. The authors estimate that eventually, these living technologies will be up to 10,000 times more effective than conventional technologies. In terms of energy and chemical inputs, the existing examples are already ten to one hundred times more effective.

We have included a few photographs of living machines with the chapter, because we feel that their strong aesthetic appeal will prove as important to their success as the fascinating theory behind them and their amazing economic performance. Being machines, gardens, and works of art all rolled into one, living machines are major milestones on the road toward sustainability.

The innumerable and life-endangering environmental ills that currently plague us globally and locally are the byproducts of human cultures and technologies deeply estranged from the great natural systems of the planet. These same systems are, ironically, the very processes that ultimately sustain us. Edward Wilson has calculated that humans are destroying species at an extraordinary rate and that between twenty and fifty percent of present living species will be extinct by the year 2025.[1] The only lasting solution to counter this dynamic is to recreate consciously symbiotic relationships between humanity and nature. Such relationships demand nothing less than a fundamental technological revolution designed to integrate advanced societies with the natural world.

Such a revolution is well underway. We have been involved in applied research into truly sustainable and equitable means for supporting the peoples of the world for more than twenty five years. Among the most encouraging recent developments has been the invention of living technologies that literally harness the intelligence, processes, and organisms found in nature not only to support human society but to restore damaged and polluted ecosystems. The component units of living technologies, called living machines, can be designed to produce food or fuels, to treat wastes, to purify air, to regulate climate, and to bioremediate ravaged ecosystems. Furthermore, they can do all of these simultaneously.

A living machine is a contained ecosystem made up of thousands of species of selected living organisms. Such an ecosystem is usually housed in a casing or structure, frequently a series of cylinders, made up of light-weight and sometimes light-transmitting materials. It is similar to a conventional machine in that it is comprised of a number of interrelated parts that function together to perform an assigned task. The design is based on principles evolved over millennia by the natural world in regulating the great ecologies of forests, lakes, prairies, and estuaries, and the ecosystems within ecosystems that are their component parts. Their primary energy source is sunlight. Mirroring the metabolism of the planet, living machines are driven by hydrological, mineral, and climate cycles.

It must be emphasized that while drawing on the ancient intelligence of nature, living machines are entirely new, humanly created ecosystems. In order to build a living machine, organisms from a vast range of sources are collected and reassembled in any number of combinations, some of which can prove unique. In the novel setting of the interior of the living machine, these organisms develop into populations co-existing often in unprecedented combinations or communities that quickly adapt to a given assignment. Depending on the goal of the project, the parts or living components may come from almost any region of the planet and be recombined in a rich variety of ways. Appropriate assembling is based on knowledge of the niches and the natural history of the organisms that are to make up the constituent parts, and on calculation of their individual role amid the constellation of organisms being incorporated by the designer.

Ultimately. it should be possible to design living machines that are at least four orders of magnitude more effective than conventional technologies.[2] In terms of energy and external chemical inputs, our recently developed waste treatment technologies are already two to three orders of magnitude more effective than existing, conventional methods.[3]

Much of the early research in living technologies was undertaken to reverse and transform the alarming and worsening state of the world's waters. All over the earth, we have poured into formerly pristine waters such toxins as fertilizer runoff and industrial, chemical, and human wastes. Countless species of fish, molluscs, frogs, and

165

Living filters for the final polishing of the purified sewage. Photo by John Todd.

amphibians generally are or are becoming extinct. Nor are these the only species at risk. In spewing thousands of chemicals into the environment, we find many of them returning to us via the water in food chains to become embedded in the cells of our bodies and those of our children. The challenge is to develop modern support systems with the ability to rapidly reverse this trend.

Because water is fundamental to all living systems, the starting point is the transformation of water-based technologies. As a substance, water is something of a scientific freak, having the rare property of becoming denser as a liquid than it is as a solid. This property is one of the reasons life is possible here on Earth. If, like other chemical substances, the solid state were denser, lakes would freeze, from the bottom up, into great blocks of ice that would never melt. The whole planet would be a lifeless ball of ice. The waters of the Earth maintain in balance all of the chemical elements of the planet and all its gases. Water is the major regulator of climate. All land-bound life evolved from this life-giving source. Approximately seventy per cent of the human body is comprised of water. If, as the Russian biologist Vernadsky claimed, water is life, the quality of water in many ways determines the quality of life.[4] Now, however, water is becoming the source, not of life, but of illness, debilitation, carcinoma, and death.

There is, however, a way of reversing this seemingly irrevocable dynamic. Living machines, by adopting and mimicking the strategies of natural systems, have proved extraordinarily effective in detoxifying and restoring the most severely contaminated waters.[5] Based on the premise that waste is a resource out of place and that nature handles every form of waste by turning it into a resource, living machines imitate the purifying and recycling abilities of natural aquatic ecosystems. Powered by sunlight and frequently housed in greenhouse-like structures, they contain populations of bacteria, algae, microscopic animals, snails, fish, flowers, higher plants, and trees. Such living machines have proved capable of advanced water treatment without resorting to the hazardous chemicals used in most existing treatment plants at competitive costs in today's terms.

We have designed and built living machines to grow food, to heat and cool buildings, to bioremediate naturally occurring bodies of water and to treat sewage, sludge, septage, and boat wastes.[6] It is possible to apply the same kind of biological engineering to the production of high-quality biogas fuels. Living machines produce by-products that can be used in the manufacture of materials ranging from paper products to advanced composite construction materials. They can be linked together to form an engineered ecology, a living technology that can be designed to protect and restore natural environments and to support human communities.

A Comparison of Living Machines with Conventional Technologies

	Living Machines	Conventional Technologies
Energy		
Primary Sources	The Sun	Fossil fuels, nuclear power
Secondary Sources	Radiant energy	Internal biogenesis of gases Combustion and electricity
Control	Electricity, wind, and solar electric	Electrical, chemical, and mechanical
Capture of External Energy	Intrinsic to design	Rare
Internal Storage	Heat, nutrients, gases	Batteries
Efficiency	Low biological transfer efficiency in subsystems, high overall aggregate efficiency	High in best technologies, low, when total infrastructure is calculated
Flexibility	Inflexible with regards to sunlight, flexible with adjunct energy sources	Inflexible
Pulses	Tolerant and adapted	Usually intolerant, tolerant in specific instances
Design	Parts are living population	Hardware-based
	Structurally simple	Structurally complex
	Complex living circuit	Circuit complexity often reduced
	Passive, few moving parts	Multiple moving parts
	Dependent entirely upon environmental energy and internal storage systems	Energy-intensive
	Long life spans ... centuries	Short life spans ... decades
	Materials replacement	Total replacement
	Internal recycling intrinsic	Recycling usually not present Pollution control devices used

168

	Living Machines	Conventional Technologies
	Ecology is scientific basis for design	Genetics is scientific basis for biotechnology Chemistry is basis for process engineering Physics for mechanical engineering
Materials	Transparent climatic envelopes	Steel and concrete
	Flexible lightweight containment materials	Reliance on motors
	Electrical and wind-powered air compressors/pumps	Structurally massive
Biotic Design	Photosynthetically based ecosystem	Independent of sunlight
	Linked sub-ecosystems	Unconnected to other life forms
	Components are living populations	Only biotechnologies use biotic design
	Self design	No self design
	Multiple seedings to establish Internal structures	
	Pulse driven	
	Directed food chains: end points are products including fuels, food, waste purification, living materials, climate regulation	
Control	Primarily internal throughout complex living circuits	Electrical, chemical, and mechanical controls applied to system
	Threshhold number of organisms for sustained control	External orchestration and internal regulation
	All phylogenetic levels from bacteria to vertebrates act as control mechanisms	
	Disease is controlled internally through competition, predation, and antibiotic production	Through application of medicines

169

	Living Machines	Conventional Technologies
	Feedstock both internal and external	Feedstocks external
	Modest use of electrical and gaseous control inputs orchestrated with environmental sensors and computer controls	Sophisticated control engineering
Pollution	Pollution, if occurs, is an indication of incomplete design	Pollution intrinsically a by-product; capture technologies need to be added
	Positive environmental impact	Negative or neutral environmental impact
Management and Repair	Training in biology and chemistry essential	Specialists needed to maintain systems
	Empathy with systems may be a critical factor	Empathy less essential
Costs	Capital costs competitive with conventional systems	The standard
	Fuel and energy costs low	Fuel and energy costs high
	Labor costs probably analogous – still to be determined	The standard
	Lower pollution control cost	The standard
	Operation costs lower because of reduced chemical and energy input	The standard
	Potential reduction of social costs, in part because of potential transferability to less industrialized regions and countries	Social costs can be high

Living machines are fundamentally different from both conventional machines and standard biotechnologies. They represent, in essence, the inherent intelligence of a forest or a lake being applied to human ends through tasks that serve human societies. Like natural ecosystems, they engage in a process of self-design. They rely on biotic diversity for self-repair, protection, and overall system efficiency. It is their aggregate characteristic that most distinguishes

Higher plants rafted on the surface of the treated sewage. Their roots support complex aquatic communities. Photo by John Todd.

living technologies, however. People accustomed to the mechanical moving parts, the noise or exhaust of internal combustion engines, or the silent geometry of electronic devices often have difficulty imagining living machines. Complex life forms viewed inside light-receptive structures can seem at once familiar and bizarre. They are both garden and machine, alive yet contained and framed living technologies that bring people and nature together in radical and transformative new relationships.

Much of the potential of living machines to protect and enhance neighboring environments lies in their photosynthetic base. Although secondary sources of energy can be and are used for control and light augmentation, both the unique adaptiveness and economic viability of living technologies lie in their dependence on photosynthetically-based food chains. They are built with parts that are themselves living populations, often extremely diverse, comprised of hundreds of species. A primary and key attribute is that the components will replace themselves as they wear out. The life span of some populations can be extraordinary, as long as centuries if housed in suitably durable containers. Further, such systems have abilities to respond and change with variations in inputs. They have the ability to self-design. Although the task is established by the human designer, when the living machine is left to express its own complexity, it may develop biotic relationships unknown in nature, thereby expanding its options for diversity. An interesting example of self design occurred recently in a living machine treating high-strength food wastes in a desert environment when the computing controls regulating flows to the system were knocked out. As a consequence, the volume of waste entering the system exceeded the design capacity of the living machine by a factor of ten for several days. The treatment facility was overwhelmed with fats, oils, and grease. Many of the organisms, including fish, were killed. The problem was discovered on a Friday afternoon and the influent pumps were stopped. Returning on the following Monday morning the plant engineers were surprised to discover that the system had self-repaired or healed itself, digested the mess of wastes, and was ready to start in again treating new material. This was possible because refugia or small side-streams had been designed into the system. These provided habitats where organisms could survive extreme conditions then re-invade and rapidly repopulate the affected zones of the living machine. This process can occur with surprising speed. We have observed a number of examples of this dynamic aspect of ecologically engineered systems.

An important aspect of living technologies, like natural systems in the wild, is that they are pulse-driven. Daily, seasonal, and sporadic variations stamp themselves deeply on their internal ecology. The background of pulses creates the resilience, agility, and vigor necessary for the systems to recover from external shocks, a response impossible for conventional machines. Yet another essential attribute is the presence of control species within the contained ecosystems. These species orchestrate the overall ecology. The building blocks behind the design, however, are the life histories of the organisms. It is essential to graft the evolution of living technologies onto a foundation of wide-ranging knowledge of natural history. The world is a vast repository of as yet unknown biological strategies that could have immense relevance should we develop the science of integrating the stories embedded in nature into the systems we design to sustain societies. Conservationists and preservationists rightly honor nature and struggle to protect the pristine natural areas that remain to us. The survival of civilization equally may require another fundamental step. It may be essential for us to find ways of decoding the natural world and of using its teachings to reshape and redefine our tools and technologies. Good farmers and gardeners have long had this kind of relationship with nature. With the unfolding and application of ecology it is possible to extend this relationship into new dimensions.

The development of living technologies had to await not only the advent of ecology as a discipline and source of knowledge but also the advancement of materials sciences to the point at which energy-efficient and environmentally responsive materials could be manufactured cost-effectively. The containment vessels frequently use light-weight, light-transmitting flexible materials that can be bonded and waterproofed, or that be floated on top of aquatic ecosystems.

Economically and energetically, living machines make enormous sense. They are cost-competitive in many areas of food growing and in purifying concentrated wastes. By avoiding any use of hazardous chemicals, they can be designed to be pollution-free in operation. It is anticipated that the aesthetics of living technologies, in addition to their functional and economic soundness, will hasten their acceptance. They can be designed to be beautiful and evocative of the deep harmonies found in nature. New economies that are an outgrowth of the wisdom and resilience of the natural world would create a new and hopeful dimension for the future.

Living machines need not be small nor isolated from larger natural systems. Scale is not an overriding factor as living technologies, like the natural world, are made up of parts that are cellular in design. Each sub-component shares the universal attributes of organisms, namely of autonomous components fused ingeniously into interdependent associations that comprise the self-regulating whole. These include such independent attributes of life as self-repair, replication, feeding, and waste excretion dynamically balanced with interdependent functions like gas, mineral, and nutrient exchange. The same natural design principles that extend from the cell to encompass all planetary biota allow living machines to vary greatly in size. They have been designed for classroom use to exhibit the functioning of ecosystems, and for treating household wastes in containers comparable to appliances like an average washing machine and dryer. So far the largest that we have designed encompasses an area of seven hectares. Conceptual projects include living machines for providing ultra-high-quality drinking water for the city of Boston that would extend for 100 kilometers inside a greenhouse-covered canal.

Looking to the 21st century, the potential contribution of living technologies is incalculable. Although fossil fuels are necessary to manufacture the long-lived materials of which the containers and mechanical parts are made, they are not needed for ongoing use. Living machines are capable of reintegrating wastes into larger systems and of breaking down toxic materials or, in the case of metals, recycling them or locking them up in centuries-long cycles. Living machines make it possible to produce large amounts of food in urban or remote areas and, as a result, could be part of a strategy for addressing issues of inequity between peoples and regions. Some less fertile parts of the world, like the the semi-arid subtropics, would benefit enormously as the tropics are the greatest reservoirs for the necessary spare parts. By miniaturizing the production of essential human services living technologies have the further potential of releasing natural systems from human abuse. This would free nature to continue to evolve in a wild state, free from excessive human interference, greatly reducing the human footprint on the ecology of the planet. This is relevant in that the long-term survival of humanity may well be predicated on a dramatic increase in the wilderness areas that are the great repositories of the Earth's biological diversity and evolutionary heritage.

The barriers to the transition from an industrially based economy to a post-industrial ecological economy are not as great as is generally assumed. Living-machine technologies for food production pioneered by the New Alchemy Institute in the 1970s are now widely employed

**Papyrus and ginger plants are well adapted to the living machine environment.
Photo by John Todd.**

in commercial food production and some are multimillion dollar enterprises.[7] Waste treatment technologies are evolving rapidly and are already cost effective in many settings. When current environmental, medical, and social costs are computed they are already adaptive in a range of settings including tropical areas. Environmental repair technologies for the restoration of lakes and polluted waters are now more cost effective than alternatives.[8] An additional and relevant attribute of living machines is that they also can be added onto existing technologies to upgrade performance and reduce pollution. In 1994 we installed a living machine at the outfall of a secondary sewage treatment plant in San Francisco. Its function is to upgrade the quality of the water being discharged so that it can be resold and reused rather than dumped into the ocean.

Living machines also can be designed to reduce or eliminate hazardous emissions from industrial manufacturing facilities. They can readily be integrated into the infrastructures of contemporary societies. Their potential to transform the visual landscape of the industrial world has been portrayed in drawings by the architect and visionary, Malcolm Wells.[9]

Ecological technologies have the ability to transform the way we live and sustain ourselves. The challenge lies in a dramatic rethinking of the human enterprise in order to redesign it to fit the laws and the needs of the natural world. Paul Hawken in *The Ecology of Commerce* states the issue clearly: "To create an enduring society, we will need a system of commerce and production where each and every act is inherently sustainable and restorative. Business will need to integrate economic, biologic and human systems to create a sustainable method of commerce." He then goes on to say quite appropriately: "As hard as we may try to become sustainable on a company-by-company level, we cannot fully succeed until the institutions surrounding commerce are redesigned."[10] Ecology provides the foundation and living technologies the infrastructure for such redesign.

References

1　Wilson, E.O. 1992. *The Diversity of Life.* W.W. Norton, New York.
2　Todd, J. & B. Josephson. 1994. "Living Machines: Theoretical Foundations & Design Precepts." *Annals of Earth,* Vol. 12, No. 1, pp. 16–24.
3　This is best represented by the new living machine for sewage treatment designed by Ocean Arks International and engineered by Living Technologies Inc. at Frederick, Maryland. It is a U.S. Environmental Protection Agency facility for the demonstration of ecologically engineered technologies.

4 Lapo, A. 1987. *Traces of Bygone Biospheres.* Synergetic Press, London. (Translated from the Russian.)

5 Todd, J. 1992. *Chattanooga Creek Pilot Remediation Project: Report to the U.S. Environmental Protection Agency.* Ocean Arks International, Falmouth, Massachusetts. (28 pp.)

6 Todd, N.J. & J. Todd. 1994. *From Eco-Cities to Living Machines: Principles of Ecological Design.* North Atlantic Books, Berkeley, California.

7 Todd, J. & N.J. Todd. 1980. *Tomorrow is Our Permanent Address: The Search for an Ecological Science of Design.* Harper and Row, New York.

8 Todd, J. 1994. *The Flax Pond Restoration Project: 1994 Annual Report to the Town of Harwich.* Ocean Arks International, Falmouth, Massachusetts. (125 pp.)

9 Wells, M. 1994. *Infra Structures: Life Support for the Nation's Circulatory Systems.* Underground Art Gallery, Brewster, Massachusetts.

10 Hawken, Paul. 1993. *The Ecology of Commerce.* Harper Business, New York.

Afterword

12

The Next Hundred Years

Yvon Chouinard

As a young man my passion was climbing mountains, and I earned a living working as a blacksmith forging pitons. The only pitons available in the late fifties were from Europe and were made of iron. The theory was that, because the malleable iron was inexpensive and molded well into rock cracks, the pitons could be left in place for the next person.

My pitons were made of aircraft-quality chrome-molybdenum steel and could be driven even into crackless, rotten seams of granite. They could be repeatedly placed and taken out without breaking, and so were instrumental in opening up the multi-day routes on Yosemite's El Capitan, where a typical climb took eight or ten days and hundreds of piton placements. In keeping with John Muir's philosophy, I tried to leave as few signs of our being there as was possible, unlike Europeans who left pitons, slings, and cables in place for future parties.

I never intended for my craft to become a business, but every time I returned from the mountains, my head was spinning with ideas for improving the carabiniers, crampons, ice axes, and other tools of climbing. My partner and I seemed to have a gift for good design, and the blacksmith shop soon grew to be a machine shop, and then into Chouinard Equipment Company. Our guiding principle of design was a quote from Antoine de Saint-Exupéry:

Have you ever thought, not only about the airplane but about whatever man builds, that all of man's industrial efforts, all his computations and calculations, all the nights spent working over drafts and blueprints, invariably culminate in the production of a thing whose sole and guiding principle is the ultimate principle of simplicity?

It is as if there were a natural law which ordained that to achieve this end, to refine the curve of a piece of furniture, or a ship's keel, or the fuselage of an airplane, until gradually it partakes of the elementary purity of the curve of the human breast or shoulder, there must be experimentation by several generations of craftsmen. In anything at all, perfection is finally attained not when there is no longer anything to add, but when there is no longer anything to take away, when a body has been stripped down to its nakedness. (De Saint-Exupéry, Antoine, *Wind, Sand and Stars*. New York: Harcourt Brace Jovanovich, 1968, pp. 41–42).

Later on I applied the same philosophy of industrial design, simplicity and absolute reliability, to the making of clothing for climbing when we started a sister company, Patagonia. Designing from the cornerstone of a functional need focused our efforts, and customers appreciated our "hand-forged" Stand Up Shorts, *cagoules*, and corduroy knickers. As the business grew, Patagonia also became a supplier of clothing for many other outdoor sports, such as white-water kayaking, back-country skiing, fly-fishing, and sailing.

In the late sixties, we began to see that the repeated use of our hard-steel pitons by increasing numbers of climbers was in fact causing a great deal of harm to the rock. We still resisted the idea of leaving gear in place, which would bring climbing standards down to the lowest common denominator, so we developed a new way to secure anchors in the rock. Our aluminum chocks could be placed in constrictions in the cracks to provide a secure anchor yet could be put in and taken out with just the fingers. Clean climbing became the accepted style throughout most of the climbing world, and Chouinard Equipment Company was the recognized leader in innovative tools for climbing rock, snow, or ice.

In 1978 I wrote a book on ice-climbing techniques. In its last chapter, I said that ice climbing had become so sophisticated that with existing tools and techniques, a skilled climber could scale any given slope of snow or ice in the world. To add sport to progress, I wrote, we have to go back. We should start doing away with these tools and replace them with greater skill and courage. I felt that the whole idea of climbing should move away from goal-oriented technology to a place in which personal qualities like creativity, boldness, and technique were supported rather than suppressed by the tools of the trade.

I lost the desire to make ever-more complex tools merely to make climbing safer and easier. I also had increasing difficulty relating to the new indoor sport climbers, who saw climbing as a strictly gymnastic endeavor in which mountains or crags were unnecessary and sticking one's neck out was unacceptable. I began loathing the very equipment I was making, preferring to go out and do easier climbs without gear rather than harder ones with all the gear. Then, as climbing became more and more "mainstream," liability lawsuits began, and I knew finally it was time to get out of the game. The assets of Chouinard Equipment were sold to some of its former employees in a Chapter 11 proceeding, and the company ceased all operations.

Meanwhile, Patagonia was growing at such a rate that in 1991 we calculated that in 11 years it would be a billion-dollar company. We were growing the business by traditional textbook means: increasing the number of products, adding retail stores, opening more dealers, and developing new foreign markets ... and we were in serious danger of outgrowing our britches. We had nearly outgrown our natural niche, the specialty outdoor market. Our products were carried in most of the outdoor stores we wanted to be in. To become larger, we would have to begin selling to general clothing and department stores. But this endangered our philosophy. Can a company that wants to make the best quality outdoor clothing in the world become the size of Nike? Can a three-star French restaurant with ten tables retain its three stars while adding fifty tables? Can a village in Vermont encourage tourism (but hope tourists go home on Sunday evening), be pro-development, woo high-tech "clean" companies (so the local children won't run off to jobs in New York), and still maintain its quality of life? Can you have it all? I don't think so.

As a society, we've always assumed that growth is both inevitable and positive: "bigger is better," "you grow or you die." When our economies sour, as they inevitably do, we simply look for new technologies, new resources, and new consumers. In America we were always able to go west whenever we needed more breathing space or more virgin groves of trees to cut or more prairies to till. Now we hunt new export markets and new Third World sources for raw materials. Free trade is replacing the microchip as our new savior. But Third World resources are close to exhaustion, and many world economies, burdened by debt, are no longer viable dumping grounds for our manufactured goods.

When the nineties and the recession arrived and President Bush began asking everyone to spend, the country's response was different. We didn't think spending would get us out of our problems. The government can offer consumers tax rebates and give incentives to help ramp up the manufacturing sector, but someone has to want to buy the product.

In Western Europe, and among the trendsetters in the United States and elsewhere, it was clear that many people were no longer interested in shopping as entertainment and no longer were accumulating wealth as a sign of status. Just a few years ago the definition of an upscale family was a television in every room; now, it's no televisions. Movie stars have been seen driving to environmental fundraisers in Toyotas and taking off their furs and pinky rings before going inside ("stealth wealth"). Maybe everyone got out of bed one day and discovered we were nauseated by the thought of going to the mall and buying more junk we didn't need. Maybe we got tired of being called consumers instead of citizens.

What if this new attitude catches on? What if America, Japan, and France decide that the right thing to do is to reduce consumption? A European only consumes a quarter of what an American does now, so it's entirely plausible that America could realize a big drop in spending habits. Even a 10 or 20 percent reduction would be catastrophic for the economy.

The world's economies are certainly threatened by more than a change in attitude. Most intelligent people around the world have stopped denying that we have enormous problems with overpopulation, pollution, climate changes, and diminishing resources. However, we are still denying that we ourselves are the causes. We say "shame" on those Mexican or Kenyan parents who have eight or ten children, yet our two North American children will, in their lifetimes, consume fifteen times more than the same number of Third World children.

We continue to delude ourselves into thinking that technology is the answer, even though over and over again it's been proven that most of our current technologies don't create jobs, but eliminate them. Technology cures our diseases but doesn't make us healthier; it doesn't even fulfill its promise to free us from our labors and give us more leisure time. All technology has really done is allowed more of us to be temporarily on this earth – perhaps only for a short time longer.

For years I was tormented by the realization that my own company, dependent on the consumer economy, was responsible for some of this overabundance of goods. Although I'd tried in the past to limit this runaway growth, I'd always failed. So now I was faced with the prospect of owning a billion-dollar company, with thousands of employees making "outdoorlike" clothing for posers. I needed to do some soul searching so I could reconnect to my original philosophy of simplicity and quality.

My wife and I flew to Florida to meet with a business consultant who, we hoped, would help us with our future planning. Before he could help us plan, he wanted to know the reasons why we were in business. We told him the history of the company, how I considered myself a craftsman who had just happened to grow a successful business. I told him that I'd always had a dream that, when I had enough money, I'd sail off to the South Seas looking for the perfect wave and the ultimate bonefish flat. We told him the reason we hadn't sold out was that we were pessimistic about the fate of the world and felt a responsibility to do something about it. We told him about our tithing program, how we gave away a million dollars in the last year to over two hundred individuals and organizations, mostly in the environmental field, and that our bottom-line reason for staying in business was to make money that we could give to such causes.

The consultant thought for a while and then said, "Oh, I think that's bullshit. If you were really serious about giving money away, you would sell the company for a hundred million or so, keep a couple of million for yourselves, and put the rest in a foundation. That way you could give six or eight million away every year, and if you sold it to the right buyer, they would probably continue tithing as well because it's good advertising."

Needless to say, my wife and I were rattled. It was as if a Zen master had hit us over the head with a stick. But instead of finding sudden enlightenment, we were shocked and confused. Only after several months of soul searching did we realize that once again we had fallen into the trap of thinking about the result and not the process. A million or ten million dollars a year won't go far toward solving the world's problems; however (back to the Zen lesson), if you want to change government, change the corporations, and the government will follow. If you want to change corporations, change the consumers. Perhaps the real good that we could do was to use the company as a tool for social change, as a model to show other companies that a company can do well by taking the long view and doing the right thing.

I have a little different definition of evil than most people. When you have the opportunity and the ability to do good and you do nothing, that's evil. Evil doesn't always have to be an overt act, it can be merely the absence of good.

I've always believed that the key to government doing the right thing is that it base its planning and decisions on the intention that the society will be around for a hundred years. The Iroquois nations extended their planning out even further, seven generations into the future. If our government acted this way, it would not clear-cut the last of the old-growth forests or build dams that silt up in twenty years. It would not encourage its citizens to have more children just because doing so equates to more consumers. My wife and I realized that if we really believed in the rightness of such planning, then Patagonia as a company must walk what it talked.

When I think of stewardship or sustainability, I think back to when I was a G.I. in Korea and saw the farmers pouring night soil on their rice paddies, which had been in continuous use for over three thousand years. Each generation of farmers assumes responsibility for seeing that they leave the land in better condition than when they took possession of it. Contrast this approach with that of modern agribusiness, which wastes a bushel of top soil to grow one bushel of corn and pumps groundwater at a rate 25 percent faster than it's being replenished.

A responsible government encourages farmers to be good stewards of the land and to practice sustainable agriculture. But why should only the farmer or the fisherman or the forester have the responsibility to see that the earth remains habitable for future generations of humans and other wild things?

We label our governments evil, yet a society gets the government it deserves. As we deny that as individuals we are the cause of our problems, we also deny that we are the solutions. No one wants to be the first to take the "hit." It isn't going to be the timber worker who refuses to cut another old-growth cedar, or the real estate broker who votes to put a moratorium on development, or the young couple that chooses to have only one child. So where do we begin?

Doing risk sports for most of my life has taught me one very important lesson: never exceed your limits. You strive, you push the "envelope," and you live for those moments when you're right on the edge, but you never go over. We must be true to ourselves; we must know our strengths and our limitations and live below our means. I decided to try to simplify my own life, reduce my consumption of material goods, eat lower on the food chain, and work toward mitigating the damage I was causing to the earth. This was a start. But I also realized that if Patagonia tried to be what it is not, if it tried to "have it all," it would die. In the clothing field, the fastest-growing companies usually have the shortest life spans. Patagonia was over the "edge," and in order to take it back to the size it should be, we had to downsize. We started by laying off 20 percent of our employees and cutting back on projects worldwide. We also made a commitment to only grow at such a rate that we would still be here a hundred years from now.

The current American Dream is to own your own business, grow it as quickly as you can until you can cash out, and retire to the golf courses of Leisure World. The business itself is the product. Long-term capital investments in employee training, on-site child care, pollution controls, and pleasant working facilities are all just negatives on the short-term ledger. When the company becomes the fatted calf, it's sold for a profit and its resources and holdings are often ravaged and broken apart, disrupting family ties and jeopardizing the long-term health of local economies. The notion of a business as a disposable entity carries over to all other elements of society. As we at Patagonia strive to make a sustainable product (hoping to make a sustainable business for a sustainable planet), we find disposability to be our greatest nemesis.

When you get away from the idea that a company is a product to be sold to the highest bidder in the shortest amount of time, all future decisions of the company are affected. The owners and company officers see that since the company will outlive them, they have responsibilities beyond the bottom line. Perhaps they will even see themselves as stewards – protectors of the corporate culture, the assets, and, of course, the employees. A corporation is only an empty legal shield without its people. A company that intends to be around for a long time must live within its resources, care for its people, and do everything it can to satisfy its community of customers. Moreover, no business can be done on a dead planet. A company that is taking the long view must accept that it has an obligation to minimize its impact on the natural environment.

As we reassessed our operation, we realized that all of Patagonia's facilities should be involved in recycling and composting and have edible landscaping, low-energy-use power, and insulation. We should use recycled paper everywhere, even in our catalogs, encourage ride sharing, eliminate paper cups, and so forth. Could we go further? Absolutely. In Denmark it's illegal to sell nonrefillable pens. So should we eliminate all packaging? We would have to get away from buying cotton from Egypt, shipping it to Japan to be made into fabric, then to Jamaica to be sewn, then to California to be warehoused, and then to stores in New York. We needed to move toward local economies.

At the same time that we were making these long-term plans, we began an environmental audit to investigate the impacts of the clothing we make. The results are still preliminary, but to no one's surprise the news was bad. Everything we make pollutes. Synthetics like polyester and nylon, because they are made from petroleum, are obvious villains, but cotton and wool are no better. To kill the boll weevil and other insects, cotton is sprayed with pesticides so poisonous they gradually render cotton fields barren; toxic defoliants are used to permit mechanical picking. Cotton fabric is often treated with formaldehyde and various resins that control shrinkage and make the fabric wrinkle-resistant. Wool relies on flocks of sheep and goats that often denude environmentally fragile land.

"Sustainable manufacturing" is an oxymoron. It's nearly impossible to manufacture something without using more material and energy than results in the final product. For instance, in modern agriculture it takes three thousand calories of fossil fuel to produce a net of one thousand calories of food. To make and deliver a 100 percent cotton shirt requires as much as five gallons of petroleum. The average so-called 100 percent cotton product is only 73 percent cotton fiber, the rest being chemicals and resins.

Other than shutting down the doors and giving up, what Patagonia can do is to constantly assess what we are doing. With education, choices open up, and we can continue to work toward reducing the damage we do. In this process, we will face tough questions that have no clear-cut answers. What good does it do to make an organically grown T-shirt if the price is so high that no one buys it except rich people who just add it to their ongoing disposable clothes collections? Should we add a bit of synthetic fiber in a cotton fabric if it makes a pair of pants last twice as long? Which is better to use, toxic chemical dyes or natural dyes that are less colorfast and fade?

In the final analysis, we have concluded that the key word that lets us out of this "no exit" dilemma is *quality*. The most responsible thing we can do is make each product as well as we know how so it lasts as long as possible. So we build clothes that don't shrink and don't need dry cleaning or ironing, that have nonbreakable, lock-stitched buttons and heavy-duty thread and stitching.

Appendix

Essential Reading List for Executives

Lester Brown et al., *State of the World*, Norton, 1995
Lester Brown et al., *Vital Signs*, Norton, 1995
Ernest Callenbach et al., *EcoManagement*, Berrett-Koehler, 1993
Herman Daly and John Cobb, *For the Common Good*, Beacon, 1994
John Harte, *Toxics A to Z*, University of California Press, Berkeley, 1993
Paul Hawken, *The Ecology of Commerce*, Harper, 1993
Hazel Henderson, *Paradigms in Progress*, Knowledge Systems, 1991
Theodore Roszak, *The Voice of the Earth*, Simon & Schuster, 1992
George Sessions (Ed.), *Deep Ecology for the Twenty-First Century*
World Resources Institute, *The 1993 Information Please Environmental Almanac*, Houghton Mifflin, 1993